1ST EDT. 2024-2025

FUSION FUNDAMENTALS WORKBOOK
STUDENT

YOUR NAME:

....

1st Edition 2024-25

ISBN-13: 979-8-9881894-7-3 (Instructor Version)

ISBN-13: 979-8-9881894-8-0 (Student Version)

Publisher: CADclass

Written By: Edward Charlwood

Edited: Jake O Sugden & Joshua Manley

Source: Saturn V Rocket, Wikimedia Commons, Public Domain.

For information on distribution, translation, or bulk sales, contact Create@CADclass.org directly.

About the Authors

Ed Charlwood is a best-selling author, award-winning educator, and expert in CAD curricula development. He has a Bachelor's degree in Engineering & Product Design and a Master's in Education from Cambridge University.

With 20 years of teaching experience and a passion for empowering students, Ed has crafted STEM curricula for 10,000+ students worldwide.

His approach to teaching has earned him prestigious accolades and recognition, including the honor of being a Google Certified Innovator, an Apple Distinguished Educator, and an Autodesk Academic Partner. He also serves as a Fellow of the Royal Society, which recognizes people who make a "substantial contribution to the improvement of natural knowledge, including mathematics, engineering science, and medical science."

Joshua Manley is the cofounder and CEO of CADclass, coauthor of several best-selling CAD books, and an Autodesk Learning Partner. As a CNC/CAD professor and published scientist, he is dedicated to empowering makers, engineers, and educators to transform their ideas into reality. With experience as the former education director of a leading maker space, Joshua has taught thousands of students, educators, and administrators across the globe. His TED-Ed talk on bicycle physics has millions of views.

Jake O Sugden is the co-founder and CTO of CADclass, a platform dedicated to empowering future engineers and designers. As the co-author of several best-selling CAD books and an Autodesk Learning Partner, Jake brings a wealth of expertise in mechanical engineering and a lifelong passion for making. His work goes beyond writing and editing tutorials—he also produces and edits instructional videos and oversees the thriving CADclass YouTube channel. A daily user of Autodesk Fusion, Jake is a hands-on expert who blends creativity with precision, inspiring others to excel in the world of engineering and design

Table of Contents

How To Use This Book

Welcome to the multi-tool of parametric CAD software, Autodesk Fusion! Get ready to combine powerful tools and fun challenges to master transformational new design skills.

This workbook is your blueprint to augment live instruction. Students should fill in the blanks, check the boxes, do the projects, and *think*. Learning the fundamentals takes about 12 hours. Mastery takes a lifetime. Your journey starts here!

To keep track of your progress, you should check these boxes. 

When you see this **Q?**............................. write your answer on it.

Changes the view left/right or up/down
....

If you'd like to read this on a computer or tablet, visit **CADclass.org/pages/books** for a free or donation-based copy of this book and others.

If you'd like step-by-step practice projects, our book Mastering Autodesk Fusion has 27 amazing ones!

If you want to pick up a physical copy, please visit our Amazon page through the following link: **a.co/d/2c64dmA**

Coming soon... An online video course designed to accompany this Fusion Fundamentals Workbook! If you're a student learning the basics or an instructor teaching a class, this course walks you through the entire book, step by step!

With clear, engaging videos for each section, you'll have everything you need to master CAD modeling with Autodesk Fusion. Choose the student version for guided learning, or the instructor version for additional teaching tips and insights to enhance your lessons.

Stay tuned—launching soon at CADclass.org!

Now this page is complete, check this off, to keep track of progress >>> 

What is CAD?

CAD, which stands for Computer-Aided Design, offers a unique blend of creativity, problem-solving, and technical skills. By using CAD software, students can bring their ideas to life, designing everything from simple shapes to complex 3D models. In the broadest sense, CAD is any tool that helps a designer… design, on a computer.

Q? What can you create with other design software?

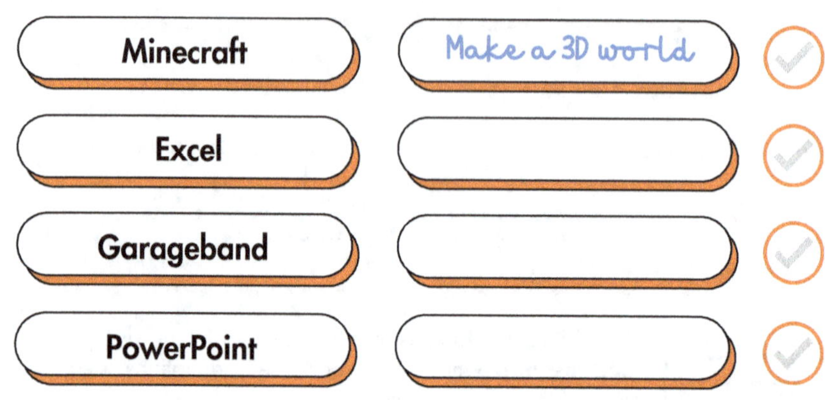

Before CAD, design was a manual, time-consuming process. Designers used drawing boards and physical tools to create blueprints, which were prone to errors and difficult to modify. Prototyping involved building physical models, making iterations expensive and slow. Collaboration was limited by the need to share physical drawings, and visualization relied on 2D sketches or scale models.

Types of CAD

- 2D (Autocad)
- 3D (Tinkercad)
- Parametric (Fusion)
- Textiles and clothing (Clo3d.com)
- Forms, surfaces and characters (Blender.org)

Q? What other examples can you think of? ....

What is CAD?

CAD stands for:

C:

A: Aided

D:

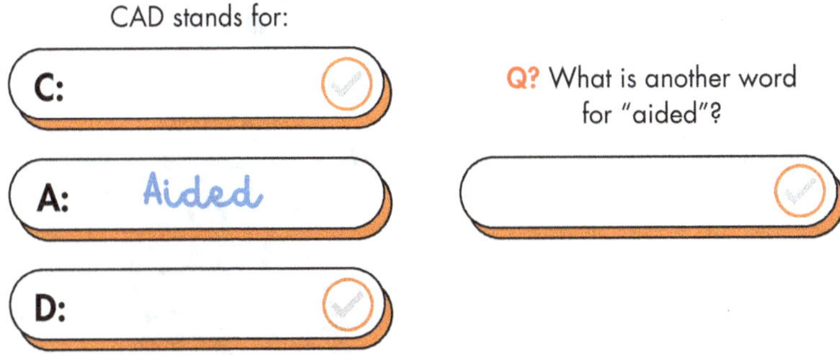

Today, CAD is ubiquitous across industries: Architects use it to design buildings and urban landscapes, Engineers it to create mechanical parts and electrical systems, Product Designers to conceptualize and prototype consumer goods... Film and Animation, Fashion, Medicine... the list is endless. While the software they use differs, the principles are the same: using a computer to help you create something. CAD is a tool of empowerment. It combines art, math, and technology. And, as you will soon see, it requires critical thinking and creative problem-solving.

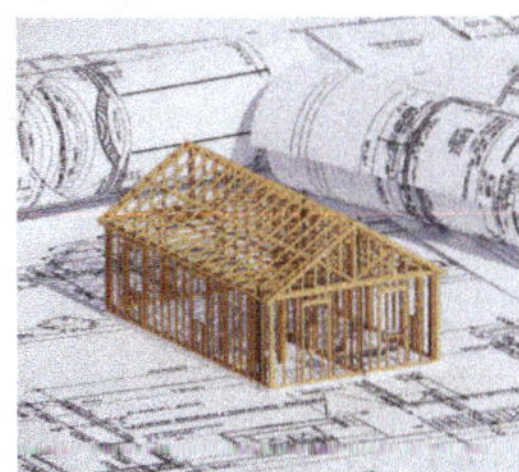
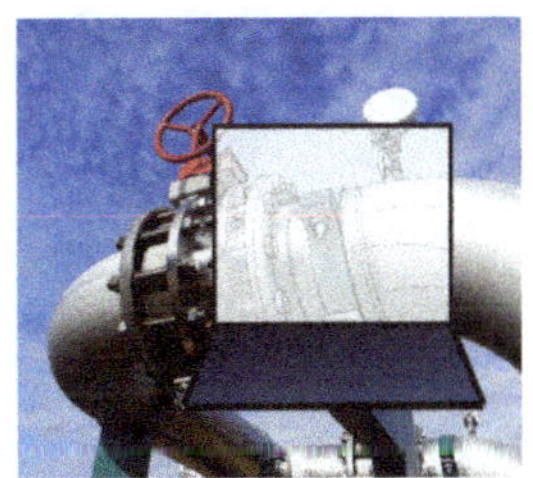

The first 747 "jumbo jet" flown in 1969 was designed using 75,000 paper drawings of 4.5 million parts, 136 miles of electrical wiring, 5 landing gear legs, 4 hydraulic systems, and 10 million labor hours: t.ly/6SRqJ

CAD revolutionized the design process. Designs are now created digitally, allowing for easy modifications and precise measurements. Virtual prototyping enables rapid testing and iteration without physical production. Collaboration is enhanced through digital file sharing and simultaneous work on designs. 3D visualization provides photo realistic representations, while integrated simulation tools allow for comprehensive analysis before manufacturing. CAD also facilitates integration with other technologies like 3D printing and CNC machining, enabling mass customization, and reducing material waste. These advancements have made design faster, more accurate, and more innovative.

Fusion is a cloud-based computer-aided design (CAD) software platform for designing models and connecting with others.

It's the multi-tool of the parametric design world, and includes 2D and 3D design, simulation, manufacturing, motion animation, rendering, and much more.

Fusion models can be 3D printed, laser cut, CNC milled, or shown to your friends and colleagues for feedback on designs.

Unlike other programs, there's no need to switch to another software to do so. It's all covered in Fusion.

Designers and Engineers are human superheroes with unique skills to improve the world. They created everything you see, hear, touch, and feel.

CAD is like having a superpower that lets you design and create anything you can imagine. So, let's master the fundamentals of Fusion a powerful tool that real architects, engineers, and designers use daily to bring their ideas to life.

Discord Community

We all have experiences of asking questions on a forum and receiving unhelpful or overly advanced responses that leave us feeling more confused and frustrated than before.

The CADclass Discord Server aims to eliminate those problems by hosting a helpful community of fellow makers with individual channels, so you can get help on a specific challenge or design problem.

Make a Discord account and sign into:

Discord.gg/5hbt6xDPqf >>

Then post your designs to the relevant channel.

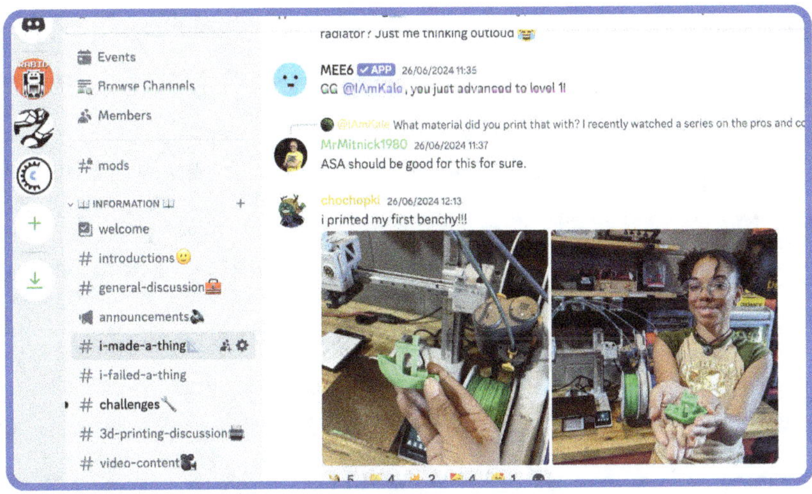

UI (User Interface)

These are the buttons for the Data Panel, File, Save, Undo & Redo.

This is where you'll find all your account details and preferences.

This is the Toolbar. It changes depending if you are in the 2D or 3D Workspace. You will tend to work from left to right.

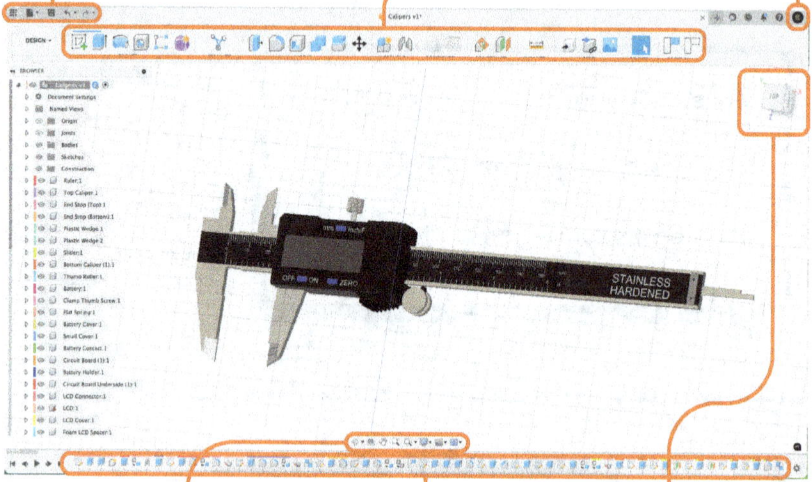

This is the ViewCube which allows you to change the view. The  icon takes you to the default home view.

The Navigation bar controls zoom, pan, and orbit for precise canvas manipulation.
The Display settings adjusts the appearance, including environment style, shadows, grids, and other view options.

This is the Timeline, a chronological list of operations. Each icon is click-able and re-order-able.

UI (User Interface)

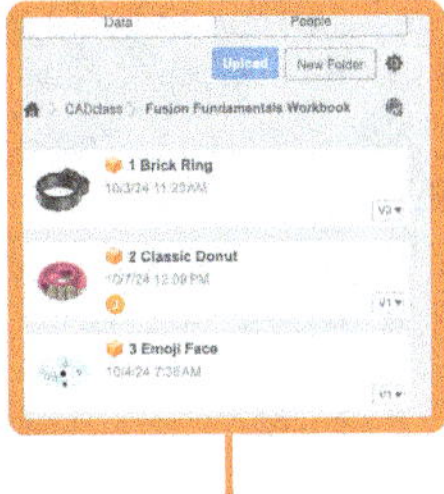

This is the Data Panel. Click the 3x3 square to see your folders and files.

You can organize your projects into different categories and add peers that you are collaborating with on a project.

These Digital Callipers are by acp5248: **t.ly/h6wiD**

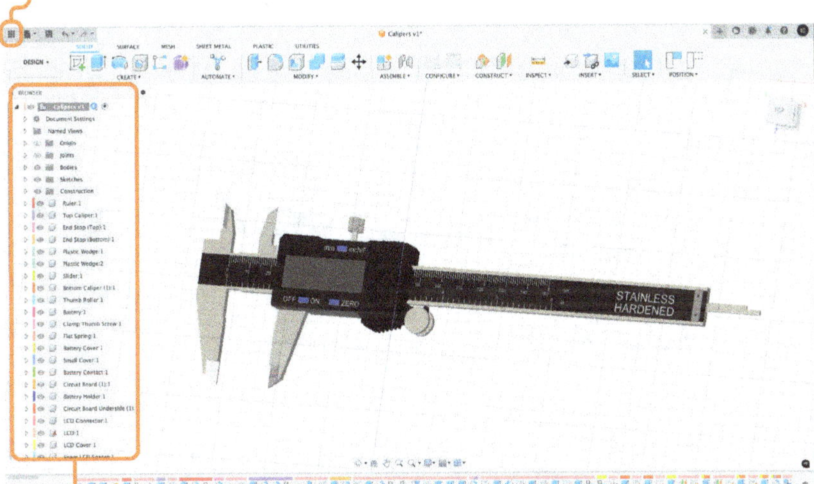

This is the Browser. It groups and lists all the subsections in a design. It includes the Origin, 3D Bodies, 2D Sketches, Joints and more.

Notice 👀 they can be expanded with the ▶ and Hidden/Shown with the 👁 icon.

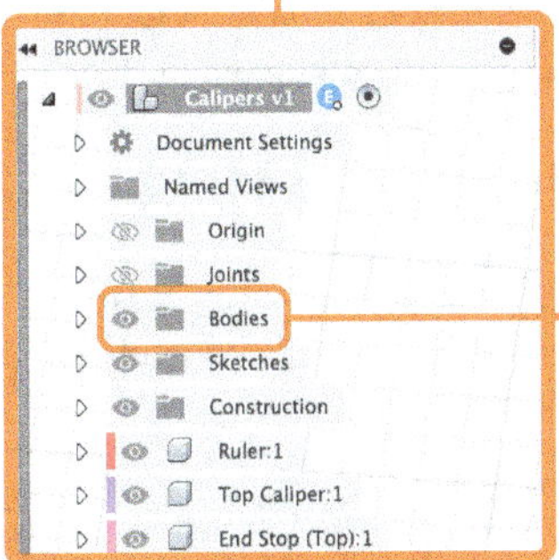

This is a folder within the Browser, specifically for 3D objects, known is Bodies in Fusion. If you make more 3D objects, they will populate here too as Body2, Body3, Body4…

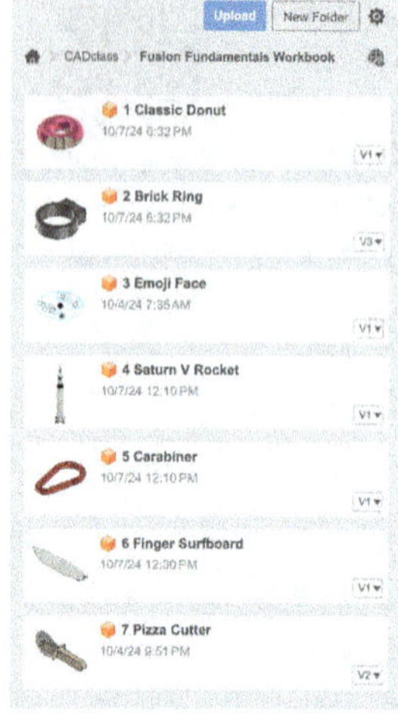

Your Data Panel is where all of your files are stored and organized. When you first open this page, you will see a series of Projects. These are the top-level organization structures that house your folders. Think of projects like your Desktop, Documents, Downloads, Pictures, etc.

Click the blue New Projects button at the top of the screen and name it CADclass. Make a Folder called Fusion Fundamentals. This is where you will save all the projects you make in this book.

Q? Click the house icon  :   What happened?

....

Open a folder and notice 👀 there is a web browser view, click on it to try it.

Fusion is a cloud-based software.

All of your files are easily accessible and sharable via your online account.

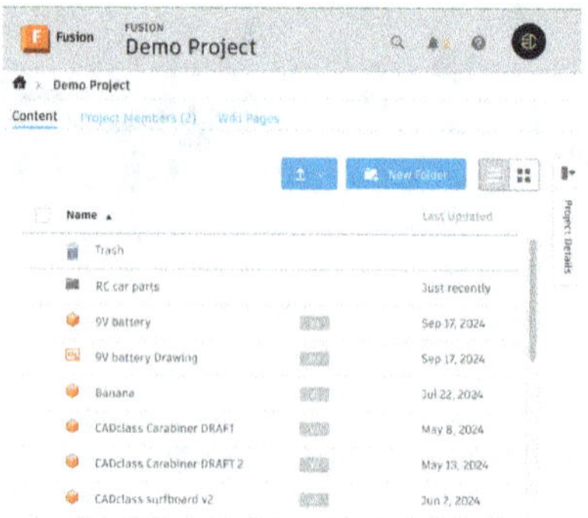

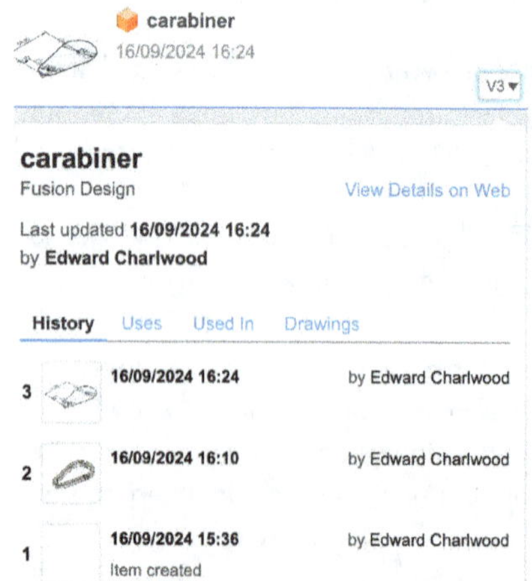

After you make a few projects and incrementally improve them, you may notice V2, V3, or V4 next to the file. These are the previous versions of your project that can be opened if needed.

Look at this example. It has a number of versions which were created every time the design was saved.

Q? How many minutes passed from V2 to V3? ....

Number The UI Features

1. Navigation Bar
2. Toolbar
3. Layout grid
4. Account

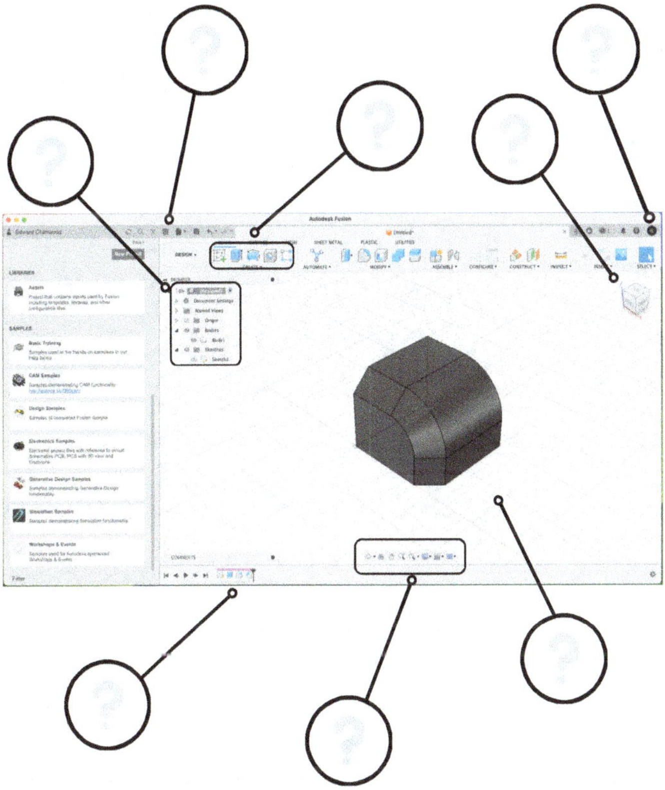

5. Timeline
6. Browser
7. ViewCube
8. Data Panel

For a free step-by-step video walkthrough visit **CADclass.org** and sign up for a free trial for the Mastering Autodesk Fusion course.

Mouse Controls

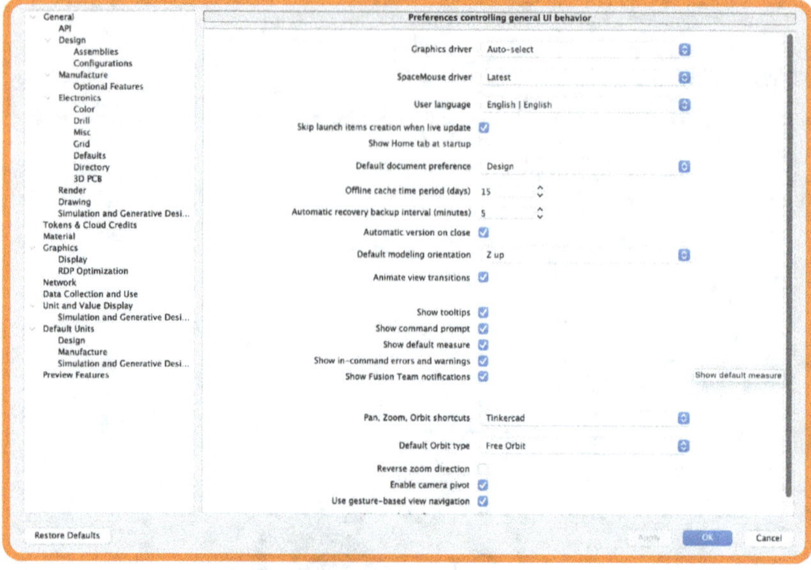

Click on your Profile icon in the top right corner and select Preferences.

Verify the **Default Modeling Orientation** is set to *Z Up* and change your **Pan, Zoom, Orbit Shortcut** to *Tinkercad*.

Q? Explore the mouse buttons.
Match them up. What does each one do?

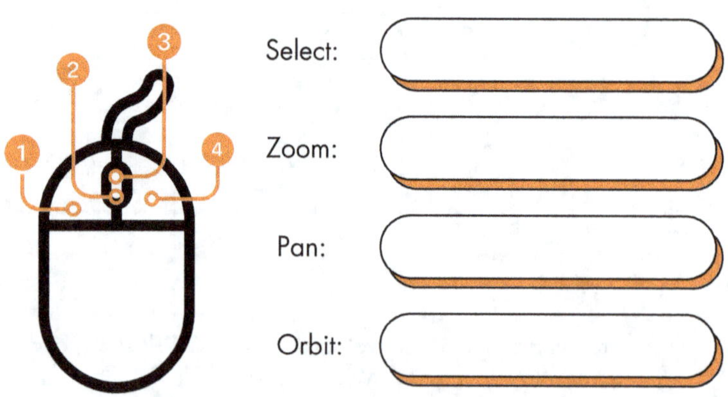

ViewCube

Label the axes (X, Y & Z):

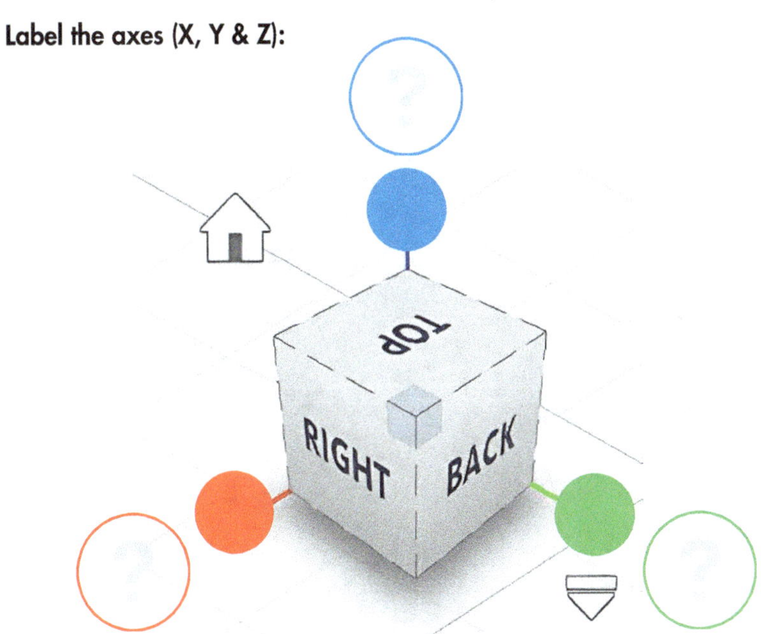

Match the highlighted feature to the name with a line:

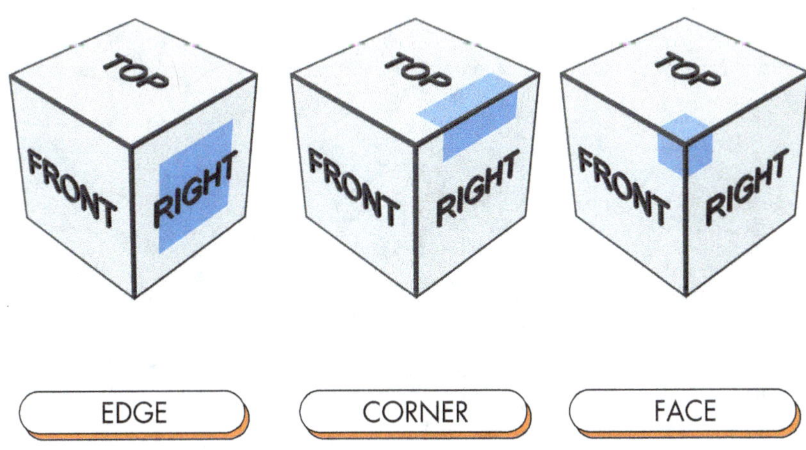

EDGE   CORNER   FACE

Planes & Axes

Define a plane in your own words:

....

Which plane is which?

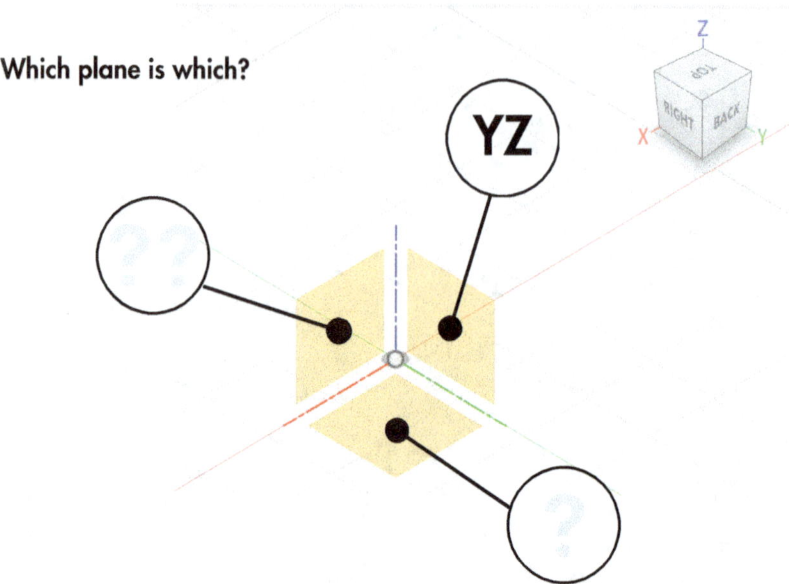

In general, it is best practice to choose the plane that logically makes your project appear like it would in real life. Designing a coffee mug standing up, not on its side or upside down, makes the most sense.

This skill may be confusing now, but it will improve as you design more projects in this book.

Intro: Classic Donut 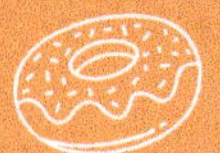

Imagine everyday objects around you, not as finished products, but as simple 2D shapes waiting to be transformed into 3D forms. With a few creative tweaks, a basic rectangle becomes a sturdy tabletop, and four elongated squares stretch into legs, giving rise to a table.

In this project, you will explore one of the most fundamental but powerful workflows in Fusion - turning a 2D flat sketch into a 3D object. With one basic shape, a couple clicks – and a few simple tricks – you will create a mouth-watering Classic Donut!

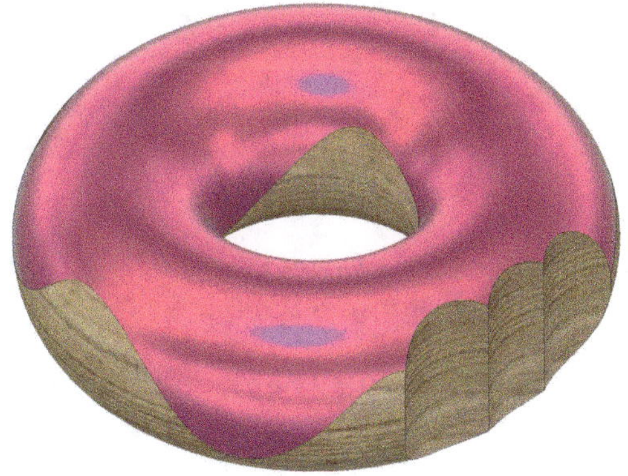

Key learning:

- Revolve a 2D Sketch around an axis to create a 3D shape
- Apply numerical value to defines a size and location of a circle
- Extrude a simple Sketch to remove (cut) away material
- Create a relationship between 2 or more Sketch entities

For a free and more detailed video walkthrough of this project, visit **CADclass.org** and sign up for a free trial for the Autodesk Fusion online course. 

Classic Donut

Click the Save icon and save the file as "Classic Donut" to the Fusion Fundamentals folder .

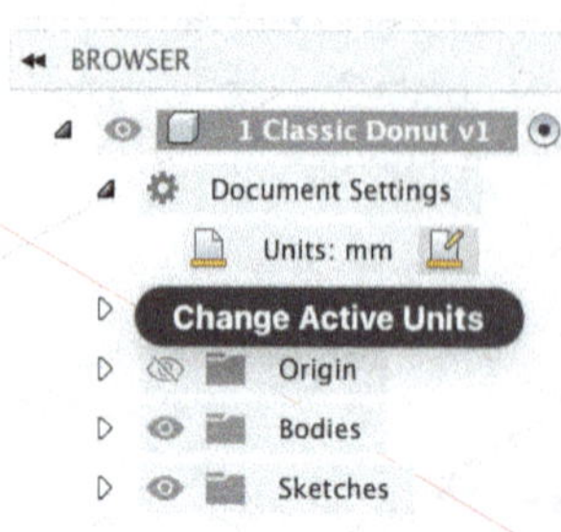

Navigate to the Browser on the left of your screen and click the triangle next to Document Settings.

Q? Are your Units are set to mm? ....

You can change them by hovering your mouse over Units: mm and clicking Change Active Units.

Start your first Sketch by clicking the Create Sketch tool in the top left corner below the word SOLID.

You have just transitioned from the 3D to the 2D Toolbar!

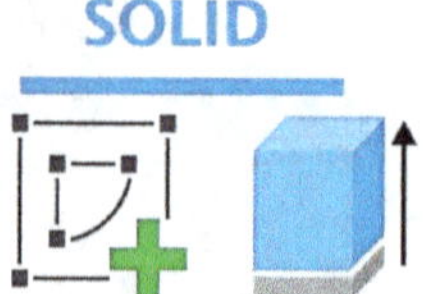

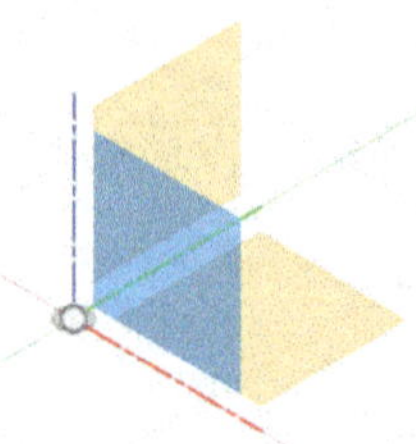

This will prompt you to click on one of three Planes. Click on the Front plane which *usually* intersects the red X-axis and the blue Z-axis. Don't worry if your colors are different.

Q? What changed about your toolbar across the top?

....

Now you are in the 2D Workspace on the Front Plane. You have a head-on view of the X and Z-axis, the canvas, and there's a gray dot in the center.

This gray dot is the Origin and is the only fixed point in the Fusion universe. Most of your sketches will reference it.

Press [C] for Circle, click to the right of the Origin near the X-axis, move your cursor up, and click again to define the circle's diameter - don't worry exactly how big it is, for now.

Press [L] for Line, click the Origin, move your cursor vertically upwards and click again. Press Esc to deselect the line tool.

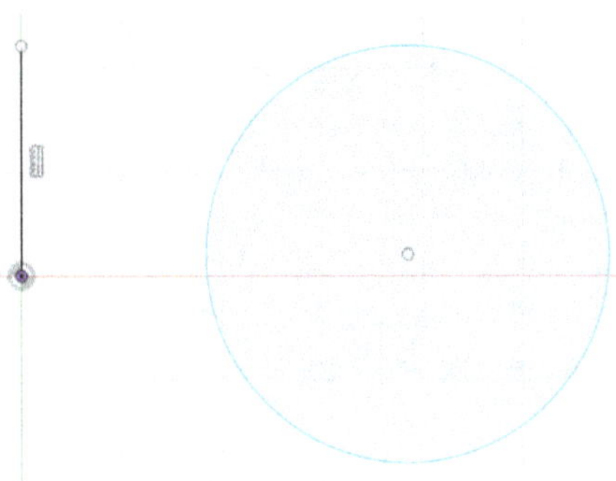

To make the Donut shape, you will rotate the circle about a vertical axis.

Because the vertical line is assisting you in making the donut shape, you can turn it into a Construction line. Click the line and press [X]. It should now be dashed.

Q? What happens if you do not press Esc after using a sketch tool?

....

To horizontally align the circle's center with the Origin, navigate to Constraints, Horizontal / Vertical constraint, and select the Origin and the circle's center.

Q? What real life object does the 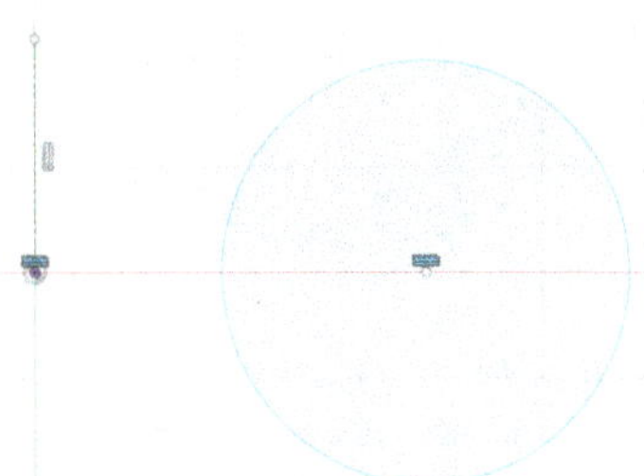 Horizontal / Vertical icon remind you of?

....

The order of operation doesn't matter with this tool. You could also click the two points in reverse order or hold down Ctrl/Cmd, select both points, and then select the Horizontal / Vertical constraint. 

Classic Donut 

Type [D] for Dimension, click on the Origin, then the circle's center, move your cursor up, click, type 40, and press Enter. This has defined the location of the circle, but not its size.

Click the circle's circumference, move your cursor away, click again, type 40, and press Enter.

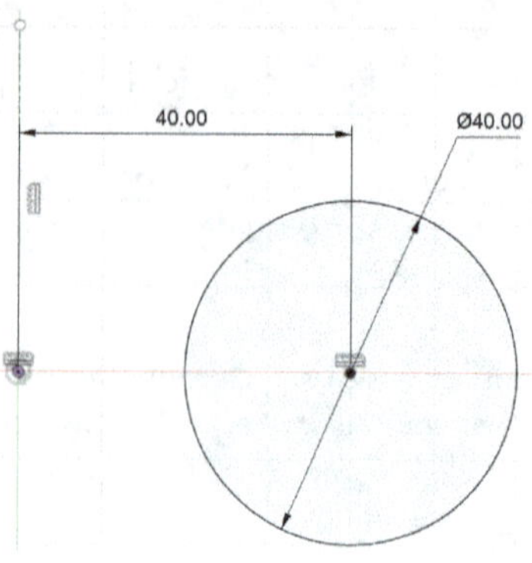

Q? What happens if you double click on the 40mm dimension?

....

Click Finish Sketch ✅ in the top right corner and click the house icon 🏠 on the ViewCube to get an Isometric view of your sketch. When transitioning from a 2D Sketch to the 3D Workspace, always have a 3 dimensional view.

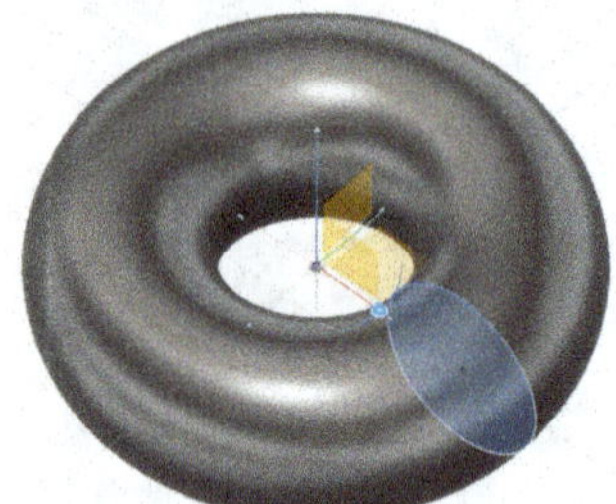

Navigate to the Create >> Revolve. The circle is auto-selected because it is the only Profile in the Workspace.

Click on the vertical Construction line to make a Torus, the mathematical name for a Donut!

You have just made your first revolved 3D object! In Fusion, this is called a Body.

Click on the triangle ▶ next to Bodies in the Browser and see Body 1. If you make multiple 3D objects in this file, they will populate here as Body 2, Body 3, etc.

Q? Which options appear if you right-click on Body 1?

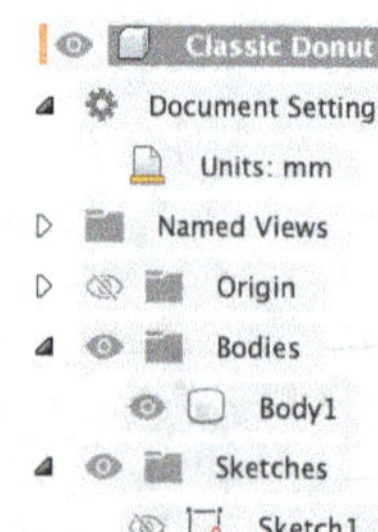

....

Classic Donut

The default appearance and material in Fusion is grey steel.

To change it, press [A] to open the Appearance tool, scroll through the material categories, expand Wood, click the download button next to Oak, and drag the Oak Cube icon onto the donut.

To edit this appearance, double-click on the Oak cube in the 'In This Design' window, and set the Scale to 44%. Click Done to close the Dialog Box.

Q? What is the maximum Reflectance value?

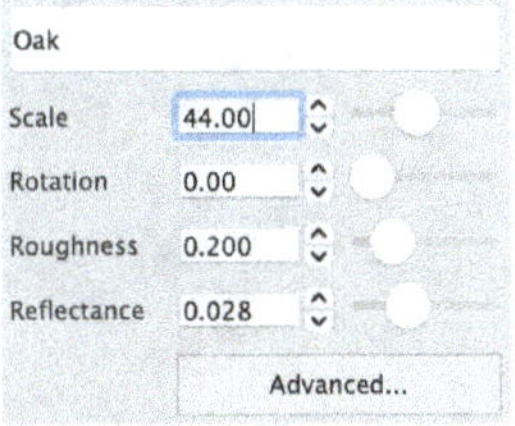

....

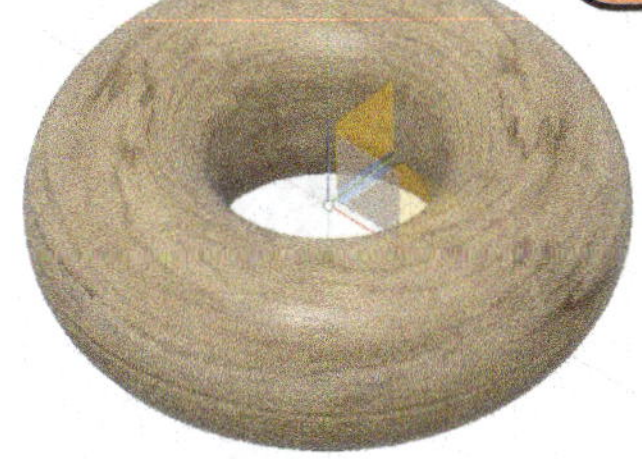

Create a new Sketch on the Front Plane, which intersects the blue Z-axis and the red X-axis.

Navigate to Create >> Spline >> Fit Point Spline, click above and below the X-axis 6 times (so the first and last points are outside the donut), and press Enter. Unlike other tools, pressing Esc will delete the spline, so you must press Enter.

Q? What happens when you move the green vertex lines?

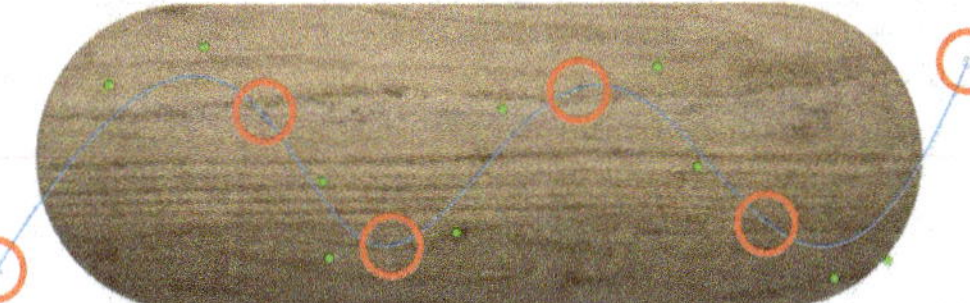

....

Classic Donut

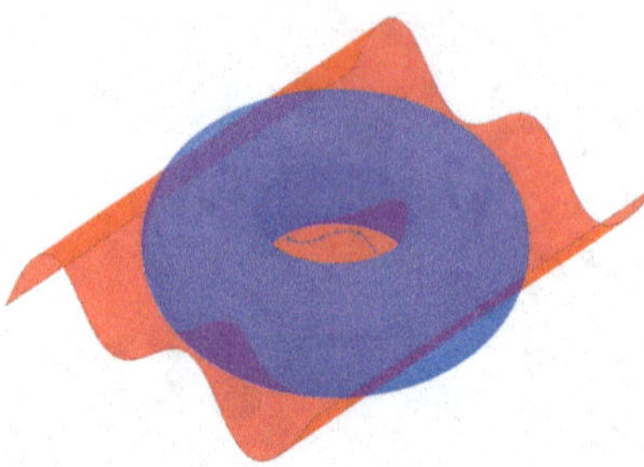

Navigate to Modify >> Split Face. Select the Donut Body, click Select next to Splitting Tool, select the spline sketch, and click OK. Sketches are often automatically hidden.

Q? What happens when you click the eye icon next to Sketch 2 in the Browser?

To take a bite out of the donut, Create a new Sketch on the Top Plane.

Type [C] for Circle and draw 3 circles near the outer edge of the donut, where the circle's centers are outside the Donut's Body and the circles overlap.

Click Finish Sketch ✅.

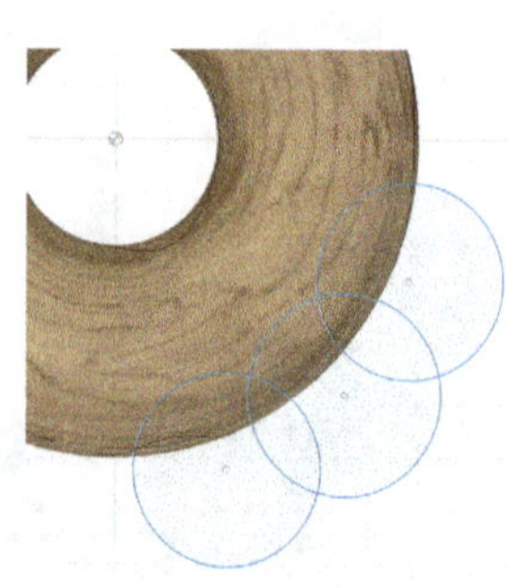

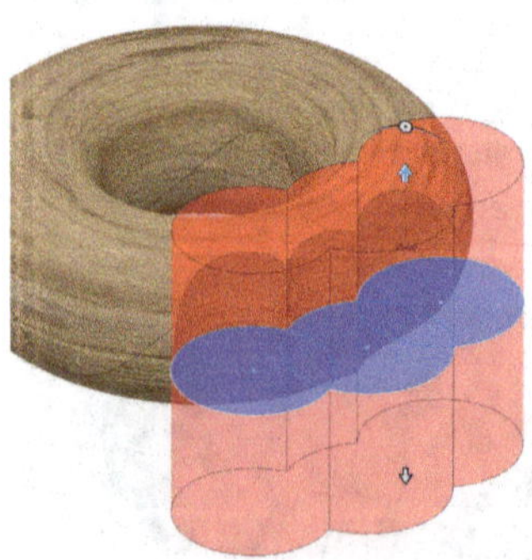

Press [E] for Extrude and select all 5 profiles that make up the 3 circles. Notice 👀 the 5 Profiles Selected in the Dialog Box.

Change the Direction to Symmetric and click and drag blue arrow upwards through the Donut in both directions. Click OK.

Q? What happens if the direction is not set to Symmetric?

To make the top half of the Donut look like dripping colorful icing, you need to add an appearance to the top face. Unfortunately, there is no premade Pink paint in the Fusion Appearances Library...so let's make a custom one!

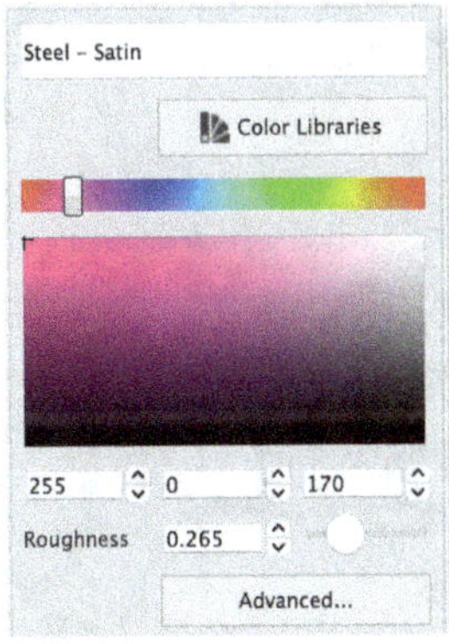

Press [A] for Appearance and double-click the Steel appearance in the 'In This Design' window.

Change the color of the steel by clicking in the color box, moving the + symbol to the top left corner for maximum saturation and moving the color slider above it until you find a **pink** color you like.

Q? What happens when you type 255 into all 3 number boxes?

....

To add the pink color only to the top face instead of the entire Body, change the 'Apply To' from Bodies/Components to Faces.

Click and drag the new pink appearance to the donut's top face. Click the Save icon 💾.

Congratulations, you are finished! 🏆

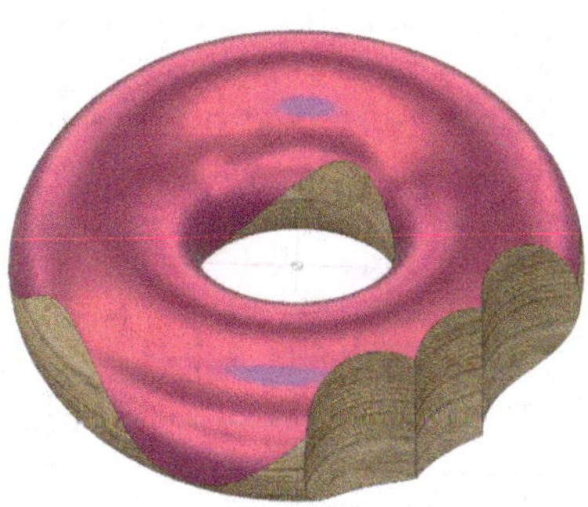

> **Review**:
>
> - To create the donut you Revolved a 2D circular profile around an axis.
> - To create the "bite" you Extrude (cut) three 2D circles from the donut
> - The workflow was from 2D sketch to 3D object

Try to re-do the Donut project in the same file with these changes:
- Make the diameter of the circle 60 mm instead of 40 mm.
- Change the distance from the Origin to 35 mm not 40 mm.

Explore these questions and try the prompts to find out what's possible:

1. Try to make the curves on the spline used to split the donut more 'extreme'.

2. Try to take a "bite" out of each side of the donut, as if it had been shared.

3. Try to make the donut have a chocolate icing topping, exploring the Appearances.

4. Double-click on the Sketch icon at the bottom in the "timeline" what happens?

5. As you click more using the spline tool, what happens to the curvature of the line you are creating?

6. What happens when you Extrude (cut) if you don't select all the circle's faces?

7. Can you enter #RGB codes when editing colors?

8. Now you have 2 split Faces, how many Bodies are listed in the Browser?

9. Which new terms can you fill out in the glossary in the back of the book?

Sketch a storyboard of how you would design, constrain, and dimension the profile of a plate to place the donut on using Sketch and Revolve.

Tool Review: Revolve

Revolve is used to create 3D shapes by rotating a 2D sketch profile around an axis. The profile becomes the cross-section of the 3D object, and the axis determines the direction and extent of the rotation. 

To turn 2D profiles into 3D objects, the profile must be enclosed. Enclosed profiles turn light blue. A common problem is a sketch profile that looks enclosed but isn't.

Shown here is an unenclosed rectangle. Can you spot where it is disconnected? In this case it's the top left corner where there are two white dots.

If you see white dots on any endpoints, even if it looks closed, it's actually a small gap.

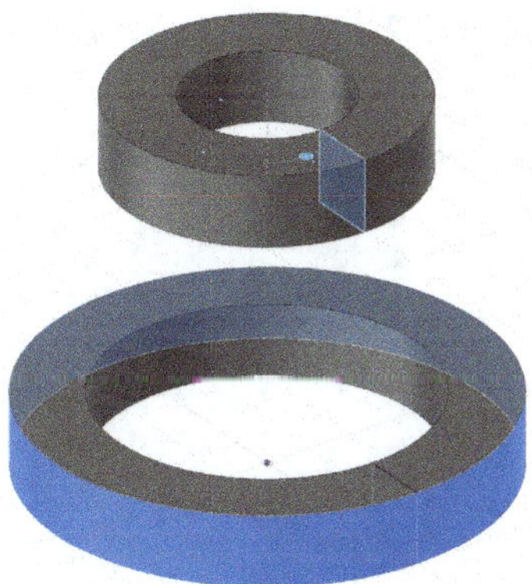

The Axis that you rotate your profile around can be the X, Y, or Z Axis, another line in your sketch, or even another round object that shares the same Axis you would like your profile to be revolved about.

Not all Revolve operations need to be the full 360 degrees, you can also set the Extent type to Partial to form a fraction of a full revolution.

You can also change the Direction so the revolve is starting from one side, two sides or symmetrically about the original profile.

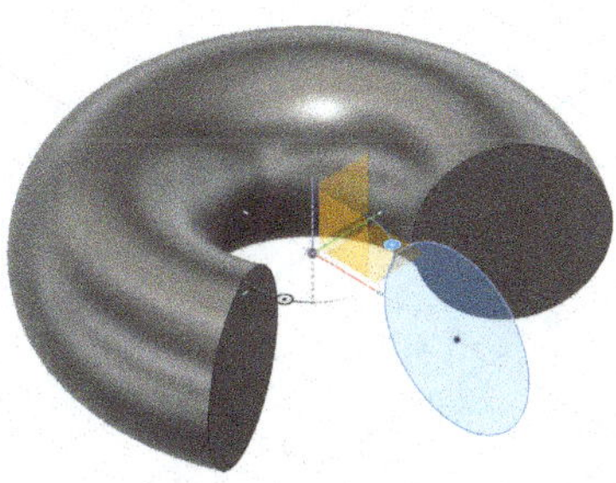

Tool Review: Dimenions

Dimensions are used for 2 main purposes, setting the exact sizes of individual parts, and defining the placement and spacing of geometry. While dimensions are essential, there are some potential pitfalls. Applying too many dimensions can lead to sketches that are visually busy and hard to read, but also almost impossible to edit effectively.

To make any dimension you need to click the line or arc, move your cursor away, click again, type the value, and press Enter.

The idea of moving your cursor away from your sketch is to keep all dimensions away from your sketch and to keep it more organized. Easily readable sketches with clearly organized dimensions are best practice.

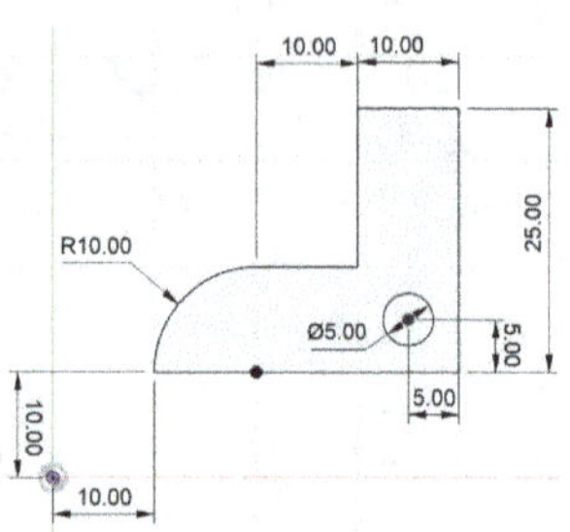

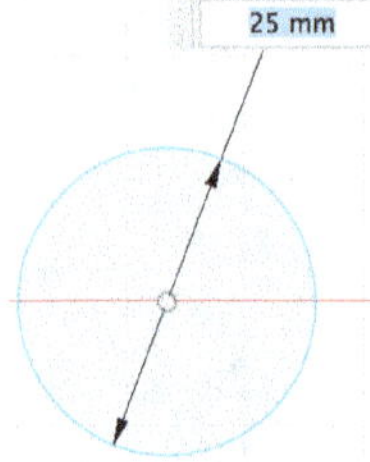

If you need to change the value of a dimension, hover your cursor over the value so it turns blue, double-click it, type in the correct value, and press Enter.

If you need to delete a dimension, click it, and press Delete.

If you have set your Units to mm, but need to add in a value in inches, or vice verse, you can type "in" or "mm" after your value, and Fusion will make the unit conversion for you, but will display it as the default document units.

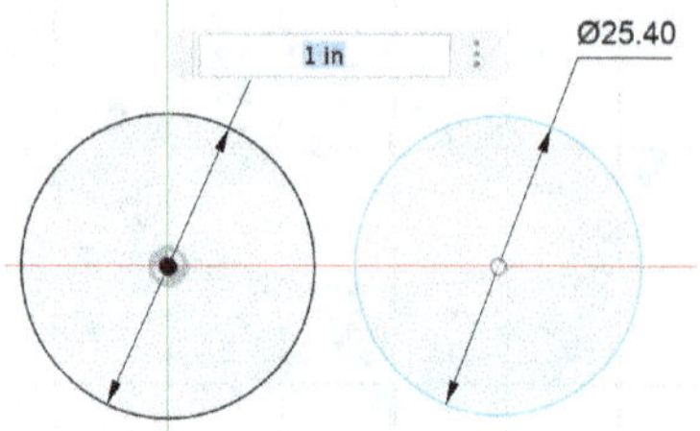

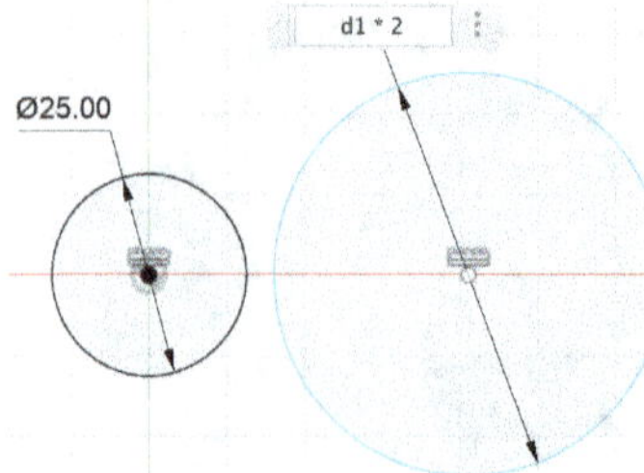

You can also add mathematical equations into your dimension. Easy math like doubling or halving the current value by adding *2 or /2 can save you a ton of time.

You can also reference other dimensions. If you want one circle to be twice the size of another, dimension a circle, click the other dimension, type *2, and press Enter.

True or False?

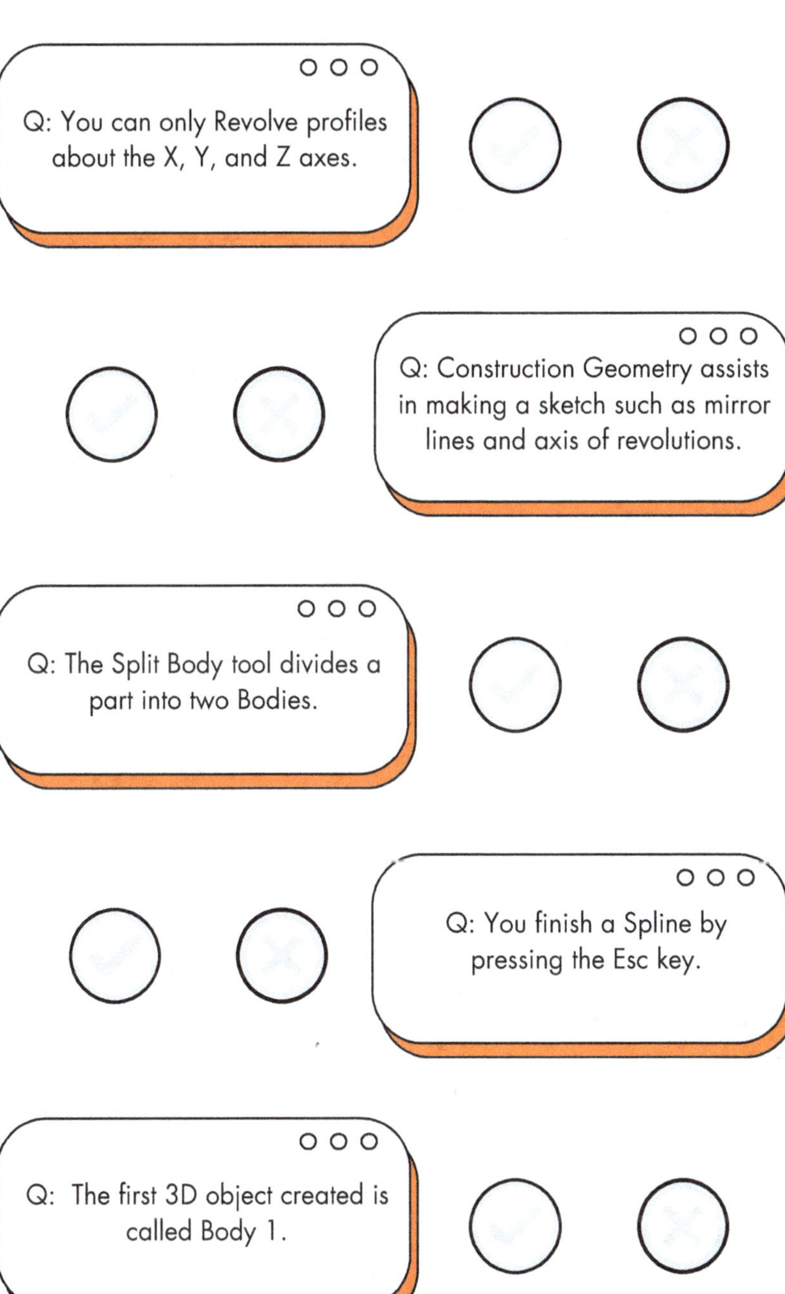

Dimension — D

Construction — ?

A — ?

? — De-select

? — E

Appearance — ?

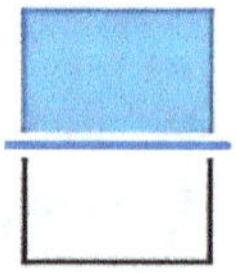

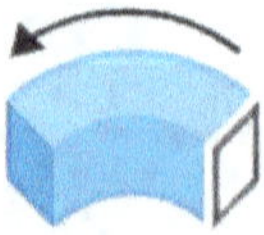

Challenge

Challenge 1:

Create a chess piece using a sketched 2D profile, starting with a vertical line from the Origin adding a series of joined-up Arcs, Lines, and Splines for the body shape.

Revolve the profile about the vertical line. Add a wooden appearance to the body and a green felt-like appearance to the bottom face.

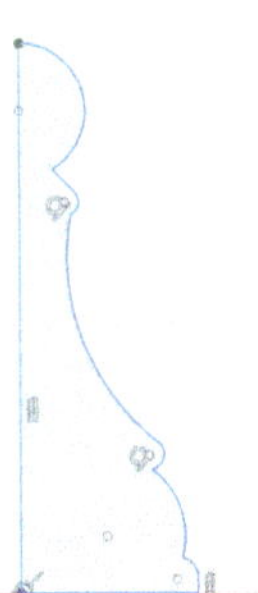

Challenge 2:

Design a colorful vase from a revolved profile.

Make the profile using Lines, Circles, Splines, and Arcs, and sketch the rough 2D shape in the box to the right.

Make a series of stacked Splines to Split the outer Face of the Body so you can color the sections different colors.

Explore styles can you make with vertical and horizontal splines.

Sketch the profile here:

Post your challenge to our Discord community:

Intro: Brick Ring 

Picture a simple ring, not just as a plain accessory, but as a foundation for something imaginative.

With a few creative modifications, a basic circular shape turns into a practical platform, designed to securely carry a small figure and bring a playful element into everyday wear.

In this section, you'll dive into the process of transforming flat 2D sketches into a functional 3D object using Fusion's essential tools.

Starting with a classic ring design, you'll learn how to create a unique, 3D-printable holder that can comfortably grip a small plastic brick or figurine with a few simple steps.

Key learning:

- Sketch and Extrude the basic shape of the Ring Body on an Origin Plane.
- Make Sketches on Faces, not just Origin Planes.
- Add Dimensions and Constraints to Sketches to keep them organized.
- Extrude cut away a cavity that can be sized to fit perfectly on your finger.
- Extrude enclosed profiles with taper angles for tight fits with plastic parts.

Brick Ring 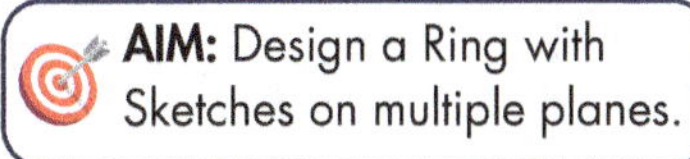

Start by clicking the (+) symbol at the top of your screen to start a new file. This opens a new tab, like in an internet browser.

Click the Save icon 💾 and save the file as "Classic Donut" to the Fusion Fundamentals folder 📁.

Expand Document Settings in the Browser and verify your Units are set to mm. All projects in this workbook are in mm.

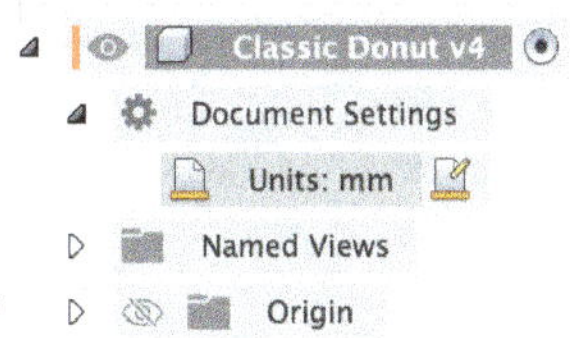

Q? Click the pad and paper icon next to Units. How many Active Units options are there?

....

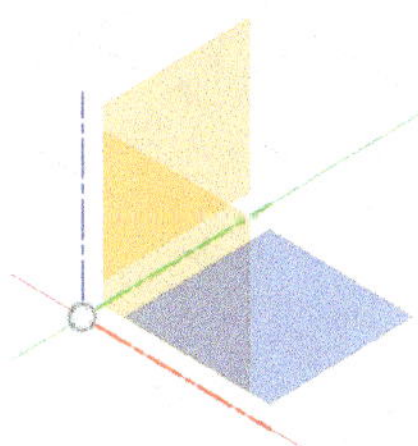

Start a new Sketch by clicking Create Sketch in the Create menu and selecting the TOP Plane which intersects the green Y-axis and the red X-axis.

Verify you selected the correct plane by checking the View Cube reads TOP.

Press [C] for the Circle tool, click on the Origin, move your cursor away, and click again to establish the circle.

Notice 👀 the Circle tool icon next to your mouse cursor. Since you don't need to make more circles, press Esc to deselect the circle tool and return to the selection tool.

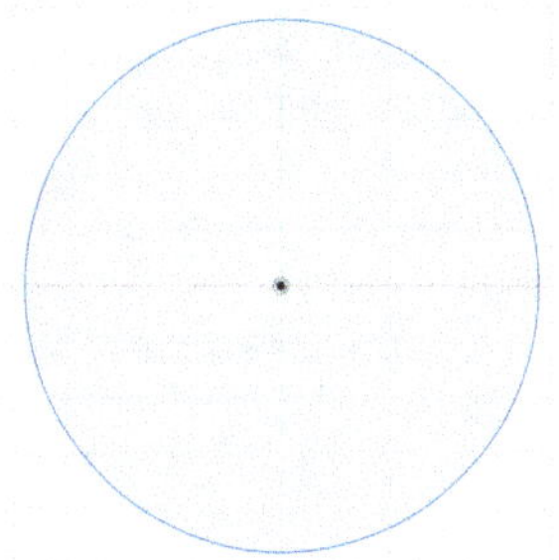

Brick Ring

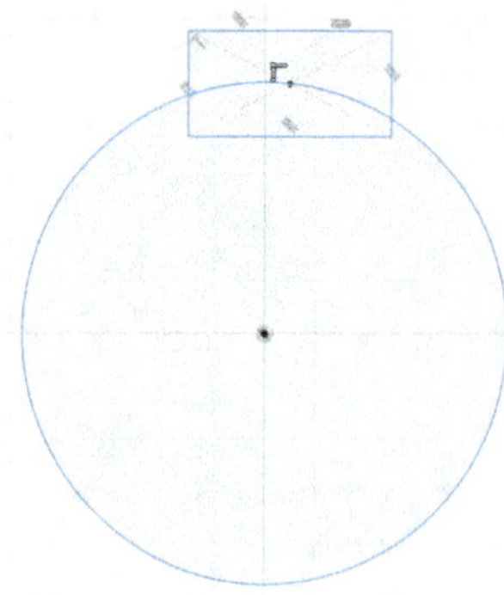

Open the Create menu to see 2D tools like lines, circles, rectangles and others. Hover your cursor over Rectangle.

Q? How many tools are there in the sub-menu to make a rectangle ? ....

Select Center Rectangle, move your cursor to the top of the circle till you see a small blue 'X', click, move your cursor up and to the right and click again.

You want the center of the rectangle to be directly above the Origin. This is done with Constraints, a set of tools that limits the movement and scale of 2D geometry so you don't need as many dimensions.

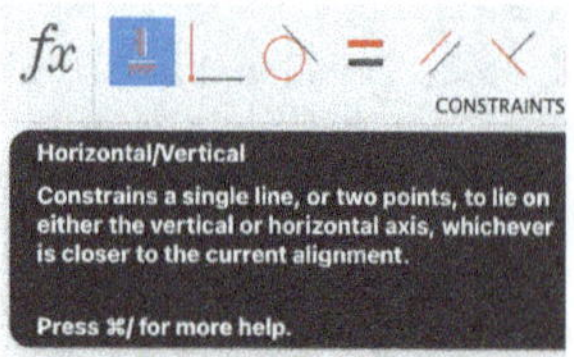

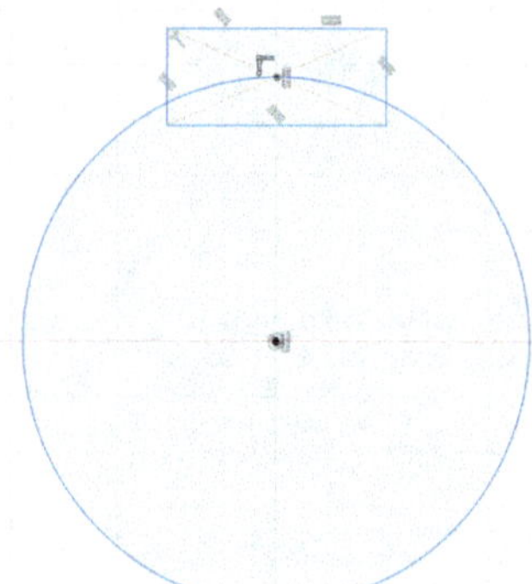

Select the Horizontal / Vertical constraint tool. Click on the circle's center followed by the rectangle's center.

Q? Click, drag and move the rectangle's center. What did the constraint do?

....

Type [D] to open the Dimension tool, click on the circle's circumference, move your cursor away, click again, type 24, and press Enter.

Click on one of the rectangle's vertical lines, move your cursor away, click again, type 6, and press Enter. Click on the rectangle's top horizontal line, move your cursor up, click again, type 15.8, and press Enter.

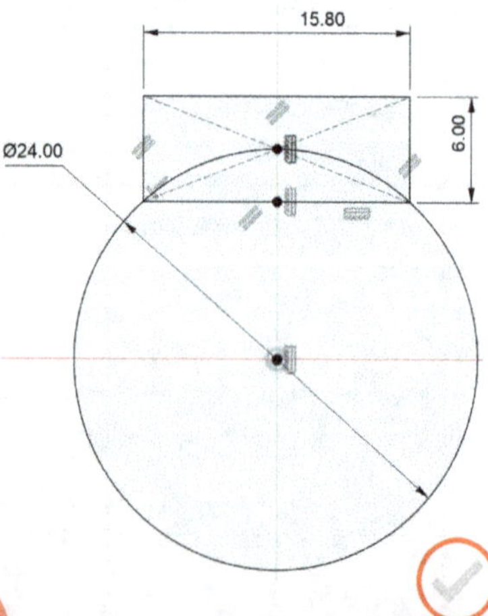

Brick Ring

Notice 👀 that the circle and rectangle were blue before adding dimensions and black after. Blue lines are Undefined, meaning the size and location of the geometry is unknown. Black lines are Defined, meaning size and location are known.

This sketch is done, so click the green checkmark in the top right corner that reads Finish Sketch to return to the 3D Workspace. In this book we will denote this step with this icon ✅.

Q? Can you move on to the next step (isometric view) if you don't Finish Sketch? How about the step after that (Extrude)?

Hover your cursor over the ViewCube and click on the house icon 🏠 above it to get an Isometric view of your Sketch.

Type [E] for Extrude, click on the 3 profiles that makes up your sketch, type 8 mm in the Distance box, and click OK.

This pop-up is known as a Dialog Box.

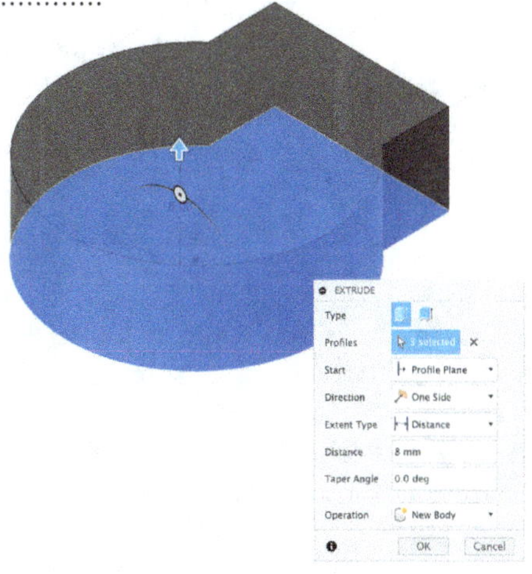

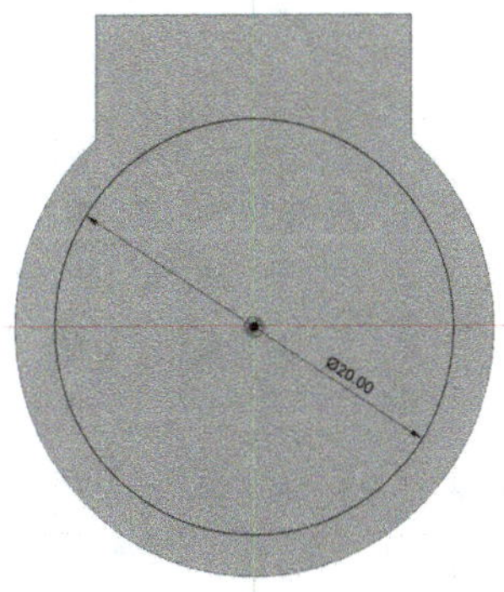

Select the Create Sketch tool, and click on the Body's top face (not a default sketch plane).

In Fusion, you can start sketching 2D geometry on the 3 Origin Planes and on the flat faces of your projects.

Press [C] for the Circle tool, click on the Origin, move your cursor away, type 20, and press Enter.

Click Finish Sketch ✅.

Brick Ring 💍

Click the house icon 🏠 on the ViewCube to get an Isometric view, press [E] for Extrude, click the circle, and set the Distance to -8 mm.

Notice 👀 the transparent red cylinder, indicating this is a Extrude-Cut operation. The Operation is also set to Cut at the bottom of the Dialog Box.

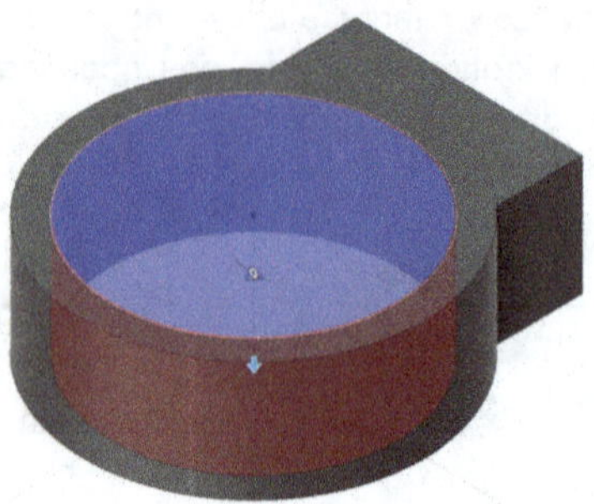

Q? Look at the Operation options in the dialog box. What other types of Extrude operations are listed?

Click and hold your right mouse button to orbit to the flat face. You can also click and drag the ViewCube to orbit but the mouse is easier.

Select the Create Sketch tool and select the flat face of the Ring.

Verify you selected the correct face by checking that the ViewCube reads BACK.

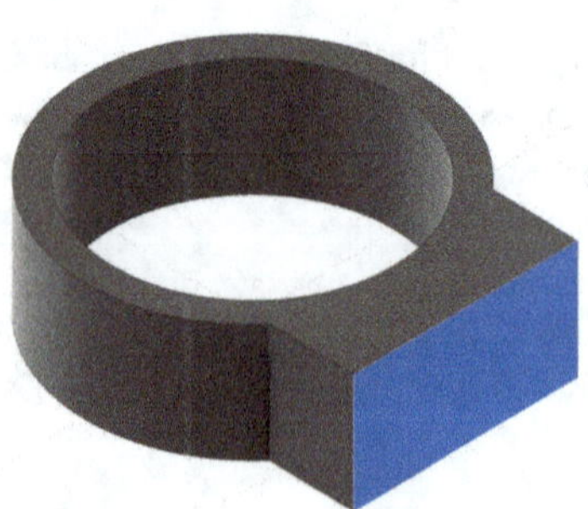

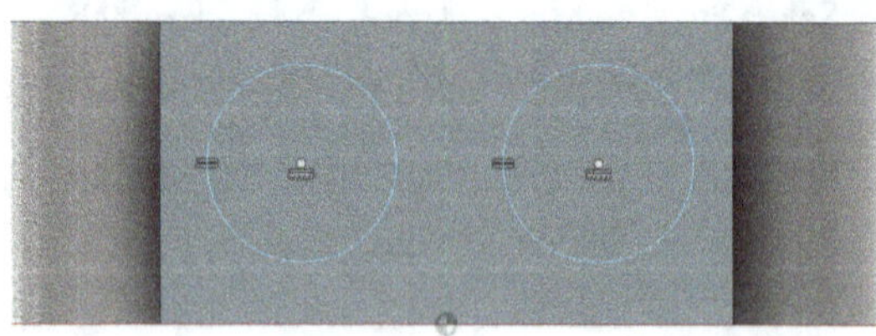

Type [C] for the Circle tool, and sketch two circles roughly equal in size.

Select the Horizontal / Vertical Constraint tool and click both circle's centers. Select the Equal Constraint tool and click both circles circumferences to make them the same size. Notice 👀 the new Constraint icons on the two circles.

Brick Ring

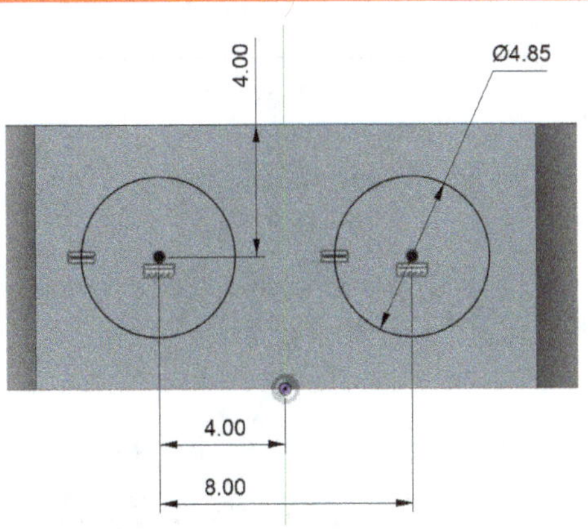

Press [D] for Dimension and add all of the following dimensions.

As you're applying your dimension, notice what happens as you move your cursor around between points (hint: orientation may change).

Q? Look in the Create menu; which of the tools (near the bottom)could have saved some effort?

....

Click Finish Sketch ✓ press [E] for Extrude, select the 2 circles, set the Distance to 2.25 mm, the Taper to -2 deg, and click OK.

The taper will make this project easier to 3D Print without needing support material.

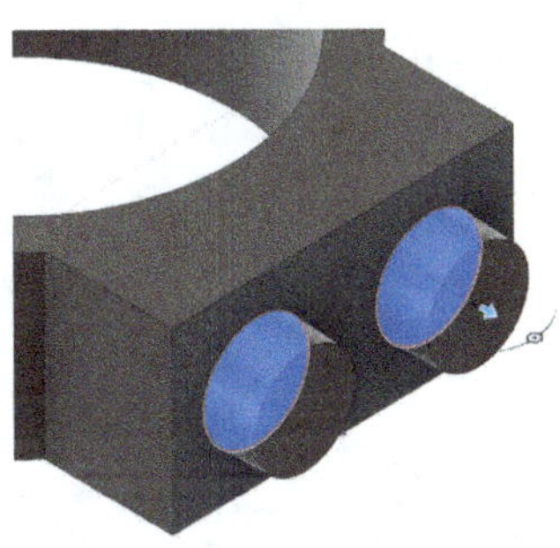

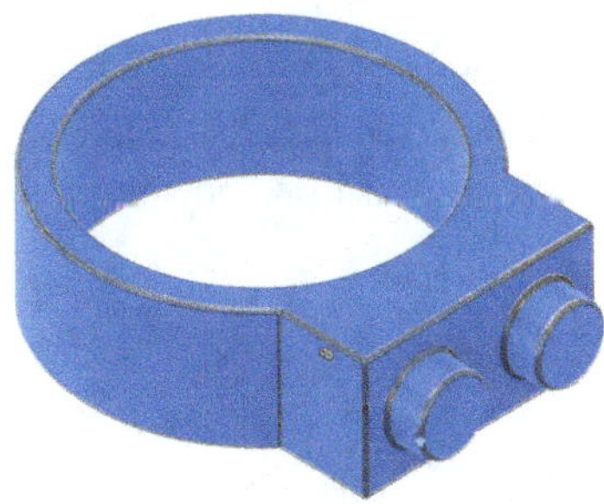

Press [F] for Fillet, highlight the entire model, set the size to 0.25 mm, and click OK. Fillets round sharp edges.

Q? What happens if you type "0.004 in" into the units box?

....

Type [A] for Appearance, search for your favorite color, and click and drag the icon onto the Body.

Done! Click the Save icon 💾.

Q? Can you save again if you don't make any design changes?

Circle the answer: YES   NO

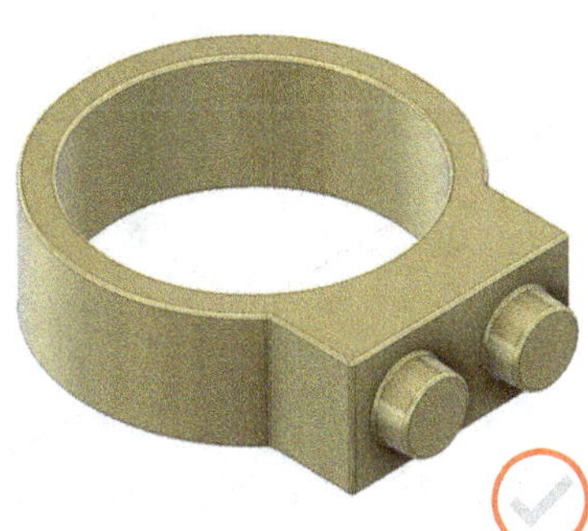

"

3D Printing

3D Printing (a form of Additive Manufacturing) is a process where a three-dimensional object is created by adding layer upon layer of material. This is done using a computer-controlled machine that can print objects from a digital design file.

The most common type is called Fused Deposition Modeling (FDM) where a plastic filament is melted and Extruded, building up the object 1 layer at a time.

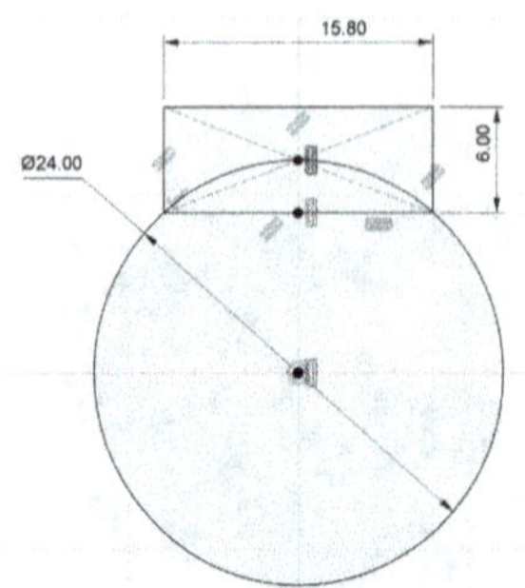

A 2D sketch...

...becomes a 3D design...

...which can be **exported** and then 3D printed!

To save your file as a 3D printable .STL, navigate to File >> Export, set the filetype to STL and download it to your desktop.

Import this file into your Slicer software of choice and print it without support material.

Slicers turn .STL files into a 3D machine-readable format called gcode.

Q? Can you export to SketchUp (.skp) from the export menu?

Circle the answer: YES   NO

Try to re-do the ring exercise from scratch but with these variations:
- Make the outer diameter circle 35mm instead of 24mm.
- Increase the wall thickness to match the original inner diameter.

Explore these questions and try the prompts to find out what's possible:

1. Try to make the outer diameter of the ring a polygon instead of a circle.

2. Instead of entering 24 mm, try typing in "0.944882 in" - what happens?

3. What happens if when you do the first Extrude, you choose the Type to be "Thin Extrude"?

4. What happens, if when you draw the 20mm circle, you set the Linetype to Construction?

5. As you Sketch and Extrude, where do these features appear in the Browser?

6. What happens if you choose Intersect when Extruding, not Cut?

7. How many directions can you Extrude in?

8. What happens if the Taper is +2 instead of -2?

9. Which new terms can you fill out in the glossary in the back of the book?

Sketch a storyboard of how you would design, constrain, and dimension the Ring to have a 4 x 4 pattern on the ring's top face?

Tool Review: Extrude

Extrude creates 3D objects from enclosed 2D Sketch profiles. It works by extending a 2D shape and adding (or removing) depth. You can specify the direction and exact distance of the Extrusion, or use other parameters like "To Object."

Toothpaste is Extruded as a cylinder when squeezed out of the round hole.

Pasta is Extruded as a tube through an O-shaped die.

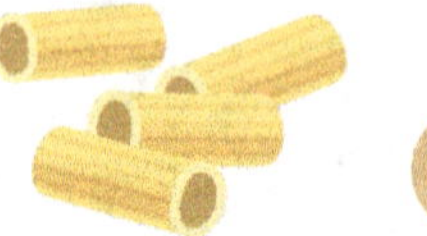
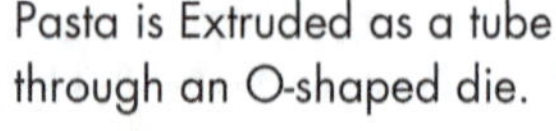

When you start to Extrude a profile, notice the blue arrow and ring icon. These are ways to Extrude and taper without needing to add strict dimensions. This type of CADing' is more freeform and is often used when the final design isn't completed.

The ring icon adjusts taper angles, negative tapers in like in the picture, positive tapers out.

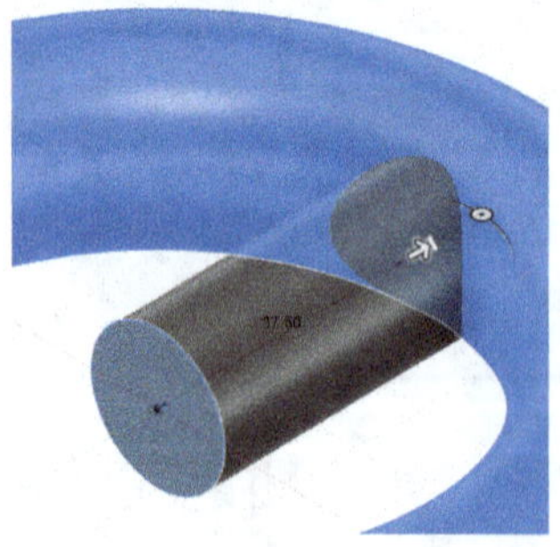

You can set the starting and ending point of your Extrusion using Start and Extent type in the Dialog Box. You can start from the profile or an offset distance from it, and you can end at a fixed distance, cut through an entire model with All, or stop when it hits another part of the design.

When extruding one profile into another, you can set what the overlapping volume will do with Operation. Join will merge the two volumes, Cut will remove the Extruded volume form the existing one, and Intersect will only keep the overlapping volume.

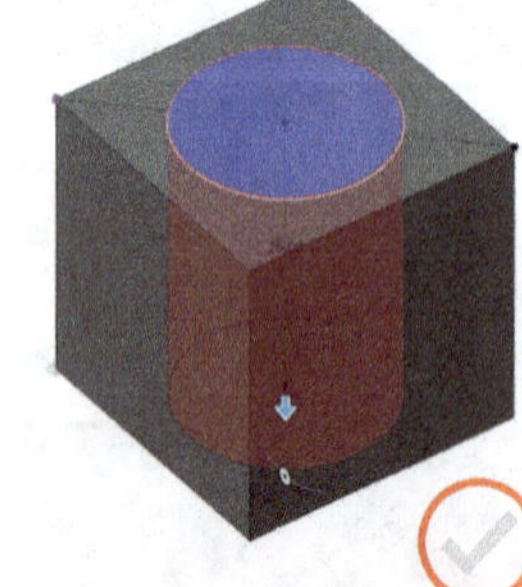

Tool Review: Fillet

Fillets create rounded transitions between edges on 3D objects, adding a radius to sharp corners, enhancing aesthetics and functionality. You can specify the radius or use options like "Constant Radius" or "Variable Radius."

You can apply Fillets, pronounced Fill-et, not Fill-ey, to edges, faces or entire bodies.

If you design a cylinder and want rounded edges, you can select both edges, or the cylindrical face.

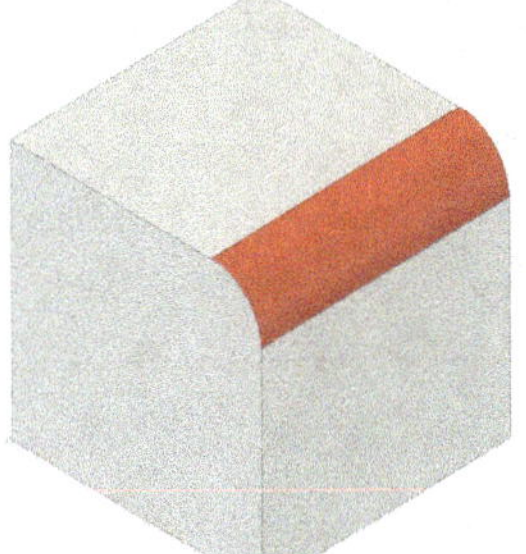

Model a 25 mm cube, type [F] for Fillet, click any edge, type 4 and this will add a 4 mm Fillet to that edge. What if you want more?

Hold down Ctrl/Cmd to get back to the selecting screen to select more.

Standard Fillets apply a constant radius to an edge, but you can also apply a variable Fillet, which changes in radius along the length of an edge.

Open the Fillet tool, select an edge, change the Radius Type to Variable, and set the Start and End radii.

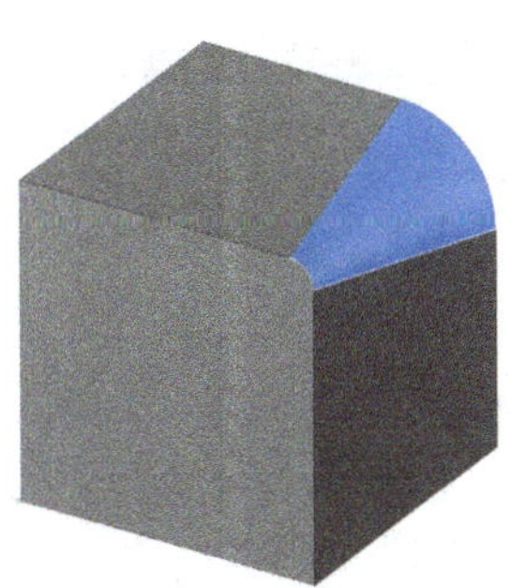

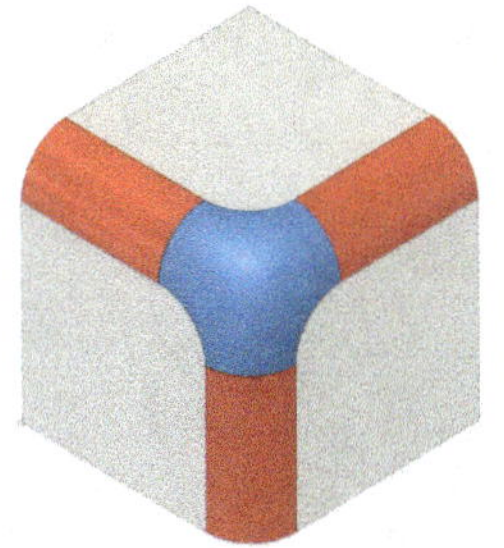

When modeling a part that requires Fillets on three meeting edges, you have the option for Setback (left) or Rolling Ball (right). They are both good options, but Setback is visually better.

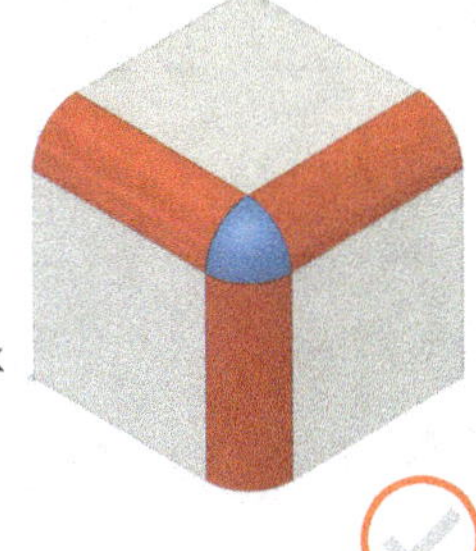

True or False?

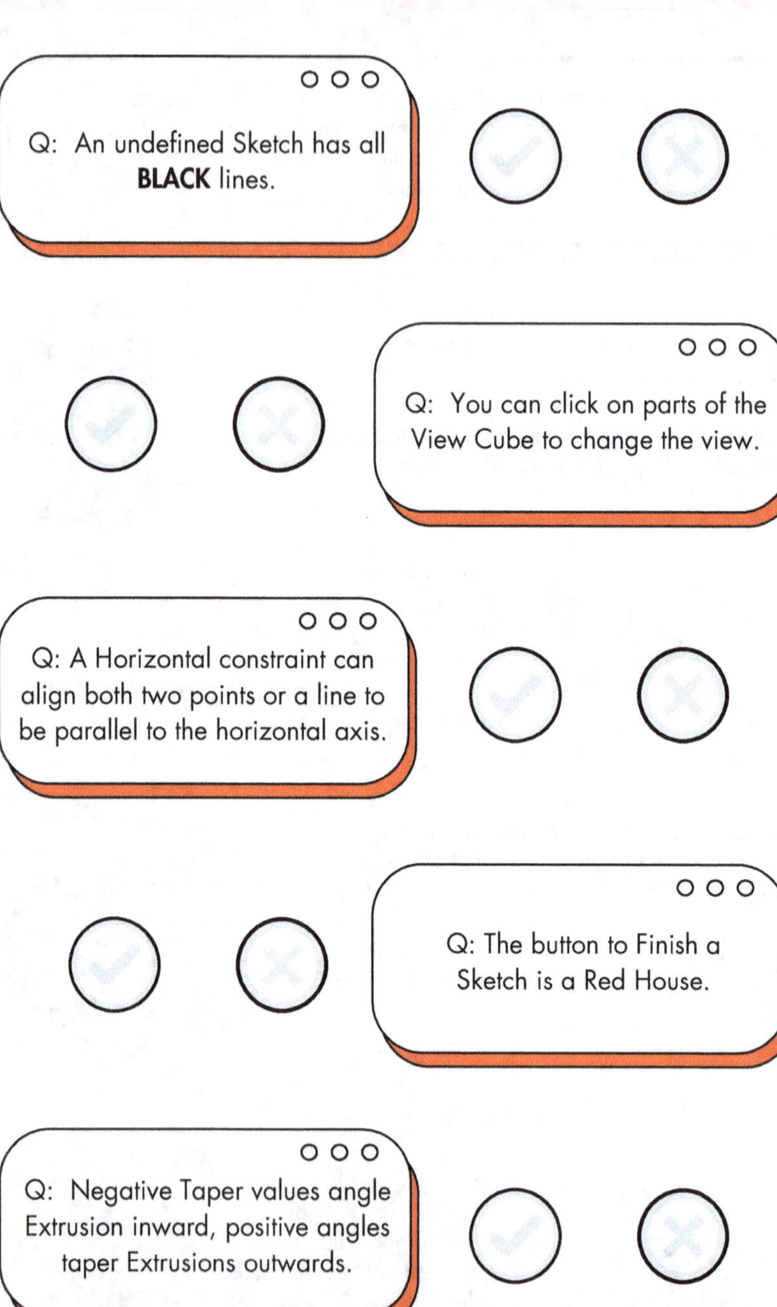

Review

Dimension	D

	De-select
	Circle
Appearance	

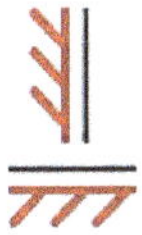

Challenge 1:

Edit your Brick Ring to make a Right with a 2x4 arrangement.

This will require you to change the thickness of the Ring, the width of the center rectangle, the pip sketch, and its Extrusion.

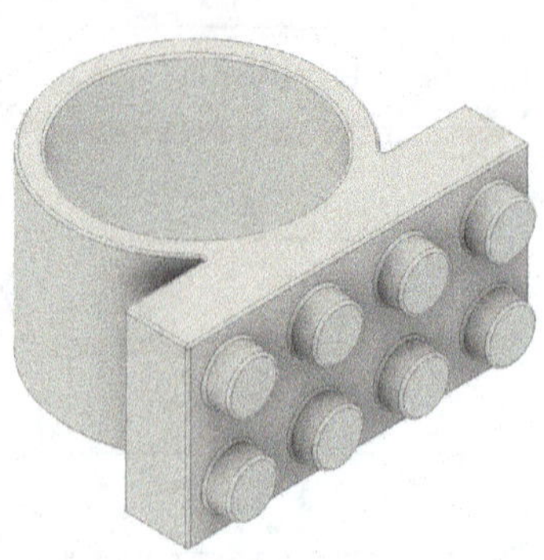

Challenge 2:

Create a block which you can attach your brick figures to accessorize your computer monitor. You'll need to think about the dimensions of the section to remove from a cuboid to slide over the top of your laptop screen.

Sketch the 2D profile here:

Post your challenge to our Discord community:

Intro: Emoji Face 😊

Mastering 2D sketching is essential because it forms the foundation for most 3D models. When sketching, it is a good practice to apply your features first and fast, then add constraints, and lastly dimensions. This technique is colloquially called 'CAD Vomit'.

Constraints define relationships between sketch elements—such as parallelism, tangency, and symmetry—while dimensions control the size and scale. Together, they ensure your sketches are accurate and adaptable.

Generally, you'll aim to use more constraints and fewer dimensions. This makes Sketches easy to read, easy to edit, and easy to understand if you need to look at it in the future or give the file to a peer.

In this activity, you will sketch an emoji to practice using a variety of constraints. You will soon see how these simple foundations turn into rockets headphones, and more.

Key learning:

- Practice fundamental workflow: Sketch, Constrain, Dimension
- Play with symmetry
- Apply constraints such as Midpoint, Concentric, Tangent, and Coincident

Emoji Face 

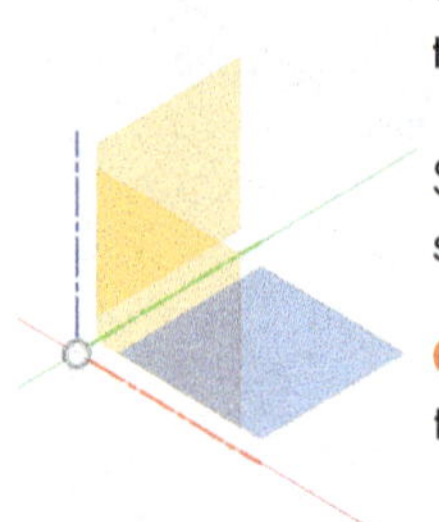

Click the Save icon and save the file as "Emoji Face" to the Fusion Fundamentals folder.

Start a new Sketch by clicking .... and selecting the Top Plane.

Q: What happens when you hold your cursor over a tool for a few seconds?

....

Expand the 2D Create tools and look at all to look at the different tools that are available when sketching.

The most commonly used tools are on the top Toolbar (line, rectangle, circle, etc) and have their own Shortcuts as capital letters (ex. C for the Circle tool) to the right of the tool.

Q? What is the shortcut key for a 2 Point Rectangle?

Write it here [   ]

Select the Circle tool, click on the Origin, move your cursor away to make a lager circle that fills up your screen.

When you start a circle at the Origin, its location is Defined but its size is unknown, meaning the entire circle is still Undefined.

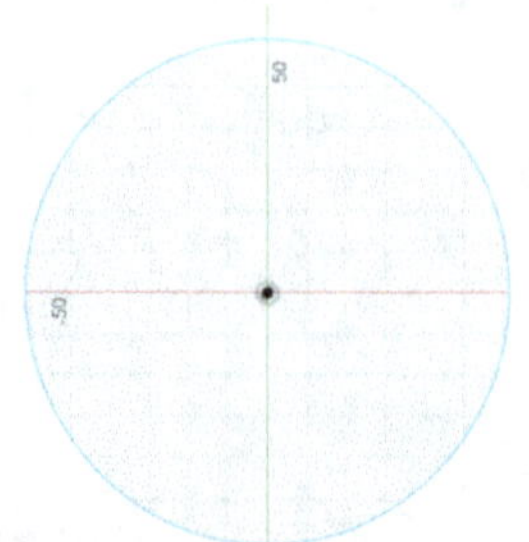
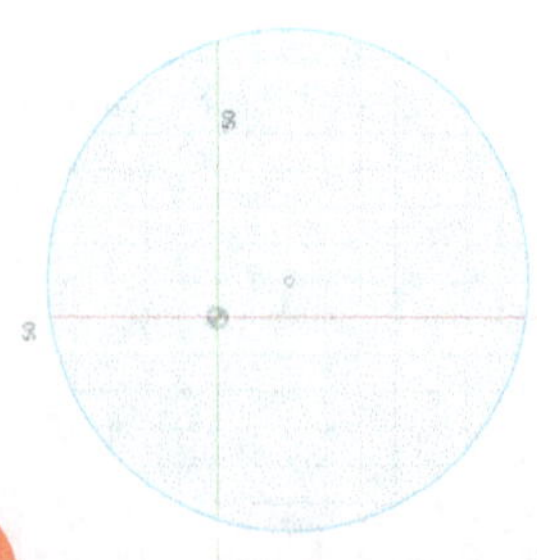

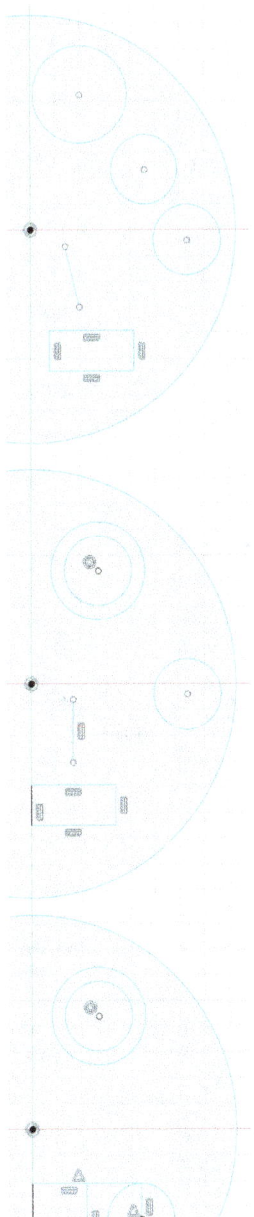

When sketching, it is a good principle to add your geometries first and fast, then add constraints, and lastly dimensions.

Draw 3 more Circles, 1 rectangle, and 1 line as shown inside the larger circle.

Select the Concentric constraint and click on the top 2 circles to place one inside the other to make the Emoji's eye.

Select the Vertical constraint and click on the angled line. If it turns horizontal, undo that operation, angle the line to be more vertical, and apply the constraint again.

Q? What does the keyboard combination Ctrl+Z / Command +Z do?

....

Select the Coincident constraint and click the left vertical line of the rectangle and the Origin.

Select the Midpoint Constraint, click the vertical line bottom endpoint, and click the rectangle's bottom horizontal line.

Click the vertical line top endpoint and click the rectangle's top horizontal line.

Click the center of the bottom circle and the rectangle's right vertical line.

Select the Tangent constraint, click the bottom circle, then click the rectangle's top or bottom horizontal line.

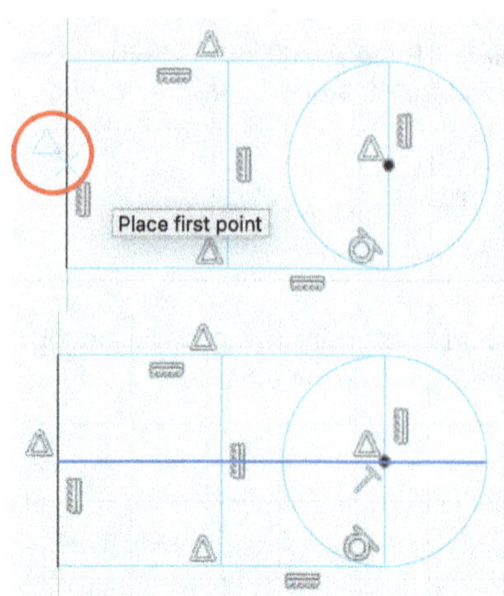

To make the horizontal line down the middle of the teeth type [L] for Line.

Move your cursor along the left vertical edge of the rectangle until it snaps to the midpoint and displays a blue triangle △ .

Click, move your cursor horizontally to the right and click on the right side of the circle.

Q? What letter of the alphabet does the Perpendicular consraint look like?

··

You can manually add constraints to Sketch features, but Fusion will also try to work out (**infer**) what constraints it thinks you want and suggest them to you with a light blue icon. This can be helpful, but you can also add them accidentally.

To make the Emoji, you need to trim ✂ away the left half of the circle. The Trim tool can be found in the Modify menu or with the shortcut [T].

Q? Which of the Modify tools in the dropdown could you use to make a feature bigger or smaller?

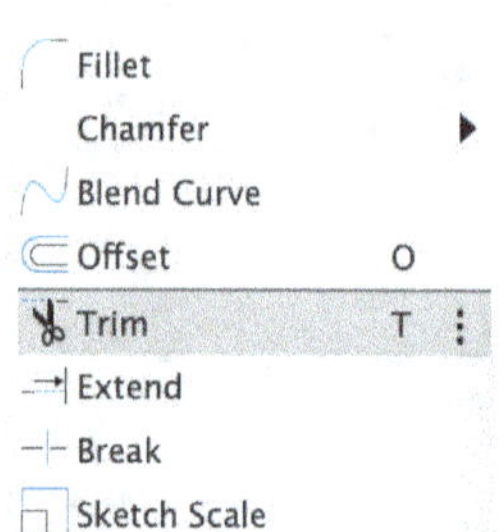

···

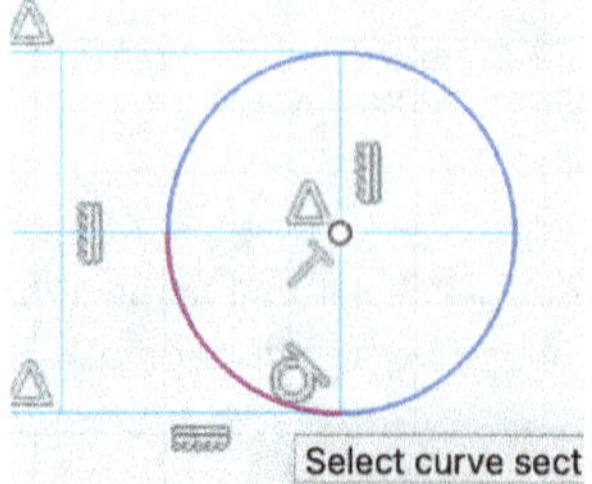

Hover over the circle's two left-hand arcs and when they turn **red** click on them or click and drag your cursor through them to delete.

Ignore the warning ⚠ that some of the constraints were removed. This is fine for now.

Emoji Face 

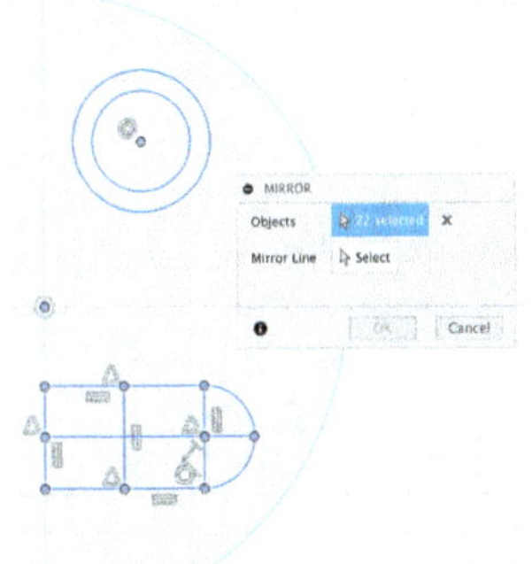

Navigate to Create >> Mirror. Click and drag your mouse over the eye and half smile to highlight them, click 'Select' next to Mirror line and select the rectangle's left vertical line.

Once you see the preview, and verify it looks correct, click OK.

Because you applied a Mirror operation, dozens of Symmetry constraints were added which can clutter your project.

Q? What appears / disappears when you uncheck Constraints from the Sketch Palette?

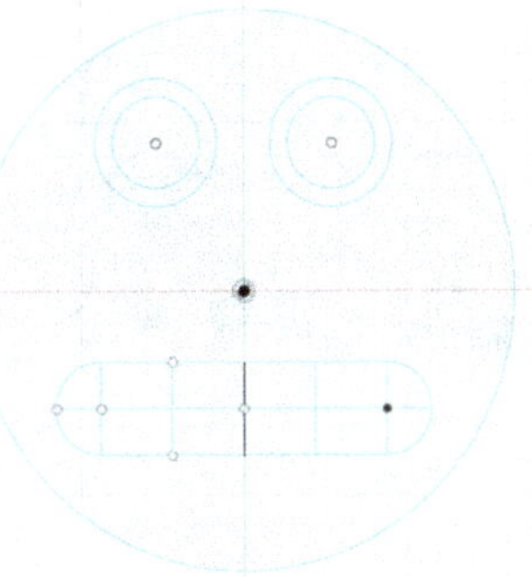

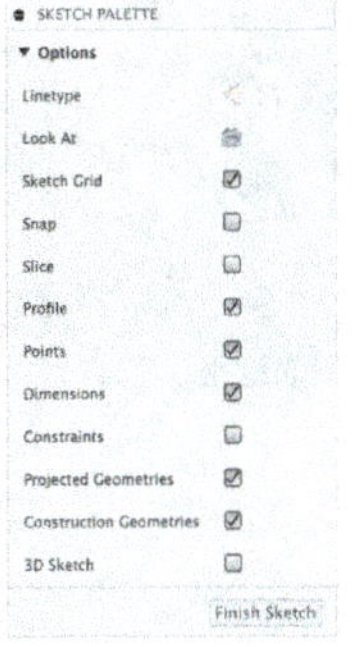

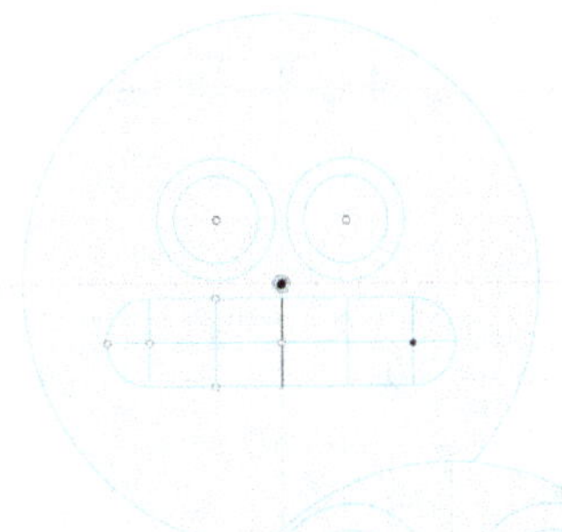

Now click, hold, and drag Sketch features from both sides. Notice how they move symmetrically because they are mirrored but that the constraints keep a sense of "order" to the design.

Click Finish Sketch and save the file.

Q? The conventional wisdom is to constrain and fully define sketches. Would you be able to move things around if you had done that?

Circle the answer: YES   NO

"

Laser Cutting

Laser cutting is a sophisticated manufacturing process that utilizes a focused light beam to cut through materials, providing precision and versatility in creating intricate shapes.

This technology has widespread use in the automotive and electronics industries Lower power (20W) machines typically cut or engrave sheet materials like plywood or acrylic, while industrial versions (1kW +) can cut steel and glass.

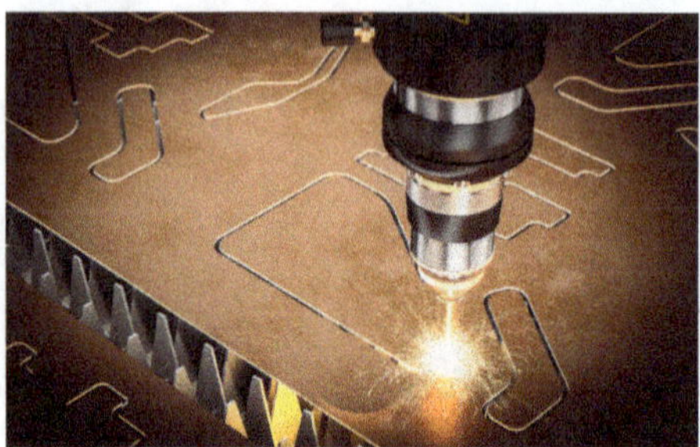

2D sketches like our emoji face are perfect for laser cutting.

Laser cutters use different file types depending on the model, but a DXF (Drawing Exchange Format) typically works.

You can also use DXF files on other 2D tools like Laser Etchers, Vinyl Cutting machines, Plasma Cutters, and Embroidery Machines.

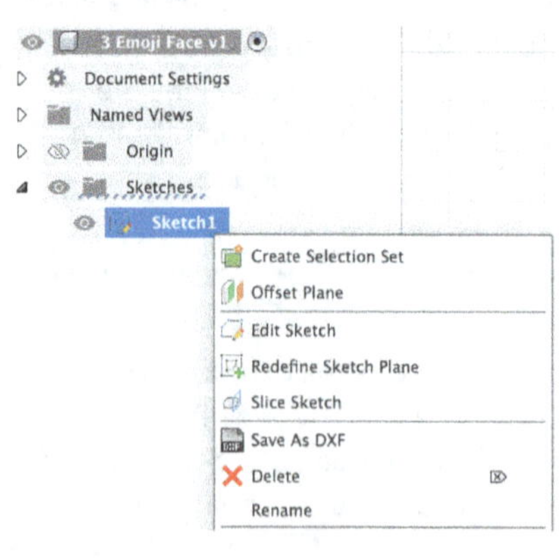

To export a laser-able DXF file from Fusion:

Navigate to the Browser, expand Sketches, right-click on Sketch1, and select Save As DXF.

Name the file and save it to your local drive.

Q? Why might it be important to rename this sketch?

Try to re-do the symmetrical Emoji Face exercise with another emoji. Practice this approach: add your geometries first and fast, then add constraints, and lastly dimensions. If you need inspiration, try one of these (easy > hard):

Explore these questions and try the prompts to find out what's possible:

1. Try to deliberately over-constraining (add too much information) and see what happens.

2. If prompted, what does changing from a "Driving vs. driven dimension" do?

3. Try remove key constraints mod-sketch, for example, to the origin, and see what happens.

4. Double-click on a dimension: what can you do?

5. What happens when hover your mouse over a constraint icon?

6. What does the keyboard shortcut [S] do?

7. Can you copy and paste sketch entities?

8. Which new terms can you fill out in the glossary in the back of the book?

Start to storyboard how you would approach creating the robot emoji. What tools could you use to create features, what and when would you constrain features?

Tool Review: Constraints

Constraints control the position and relationship between different elements in a 2D sketch. They allow CAD designers to define specific rules and conditions that govern how parts, features, and components interact.

Constraints can be used for a variety of purposes in Fusion CAD, including:

- To fix the location and orientation of parts relative to one another.
- To establish relationships between features, such as aligning edges, matching sizes, or maintaining tangency.
- To control how a model responds to changes in parameters, ensuring that the overall design intent is maintained.

While constraints are useful, there are some potential pitfalls:

- Constraints that contradict each other can cause the model to become unstable or fail to update correctly.
- Constraints can create complex dependencies between different elements of the model. Changes to one part may have unintended consequences on other parts, which can make the design process more challenging.

In some sketches, you can use two different constraints and get the same result.

You can make 2 circles that share the same center by using the Concentric constraint and clicking the circle's perimeters, or using the Coincident constraint and selecting both circle's centers.

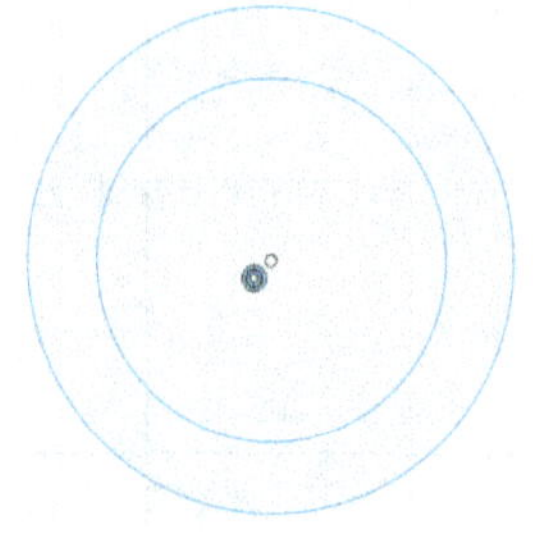

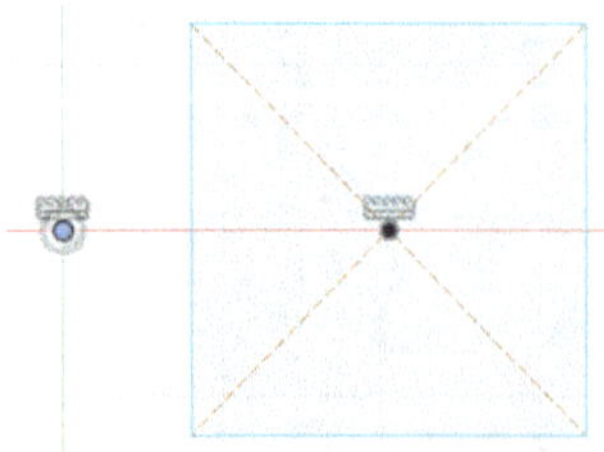

The order of operations doesn't matter for most constraints, except for Symmetric. To apply a Horizontal constraint to two points, you could:

- Select the H/V constraint, then select both points.
- Hold down Ctrl/Cmd, select both points, then select the H/V constraint
- Click one point, select the H/V constraint, then click the other point.

Constraints Review

Name the Constraints and draw the icon

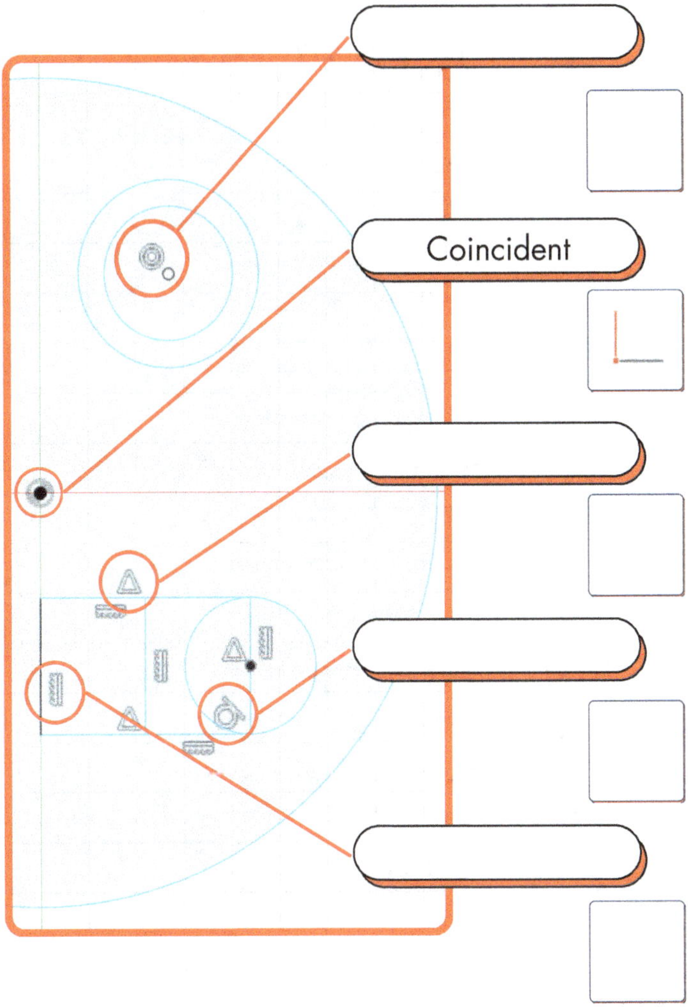

Coincident

A Dimension is a numerical value that defines the size, location, or geometry design elements. Dimensions specify measurements such as lengths, widths, heights, angles, and diameters.

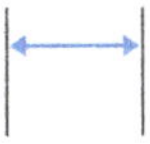

Review

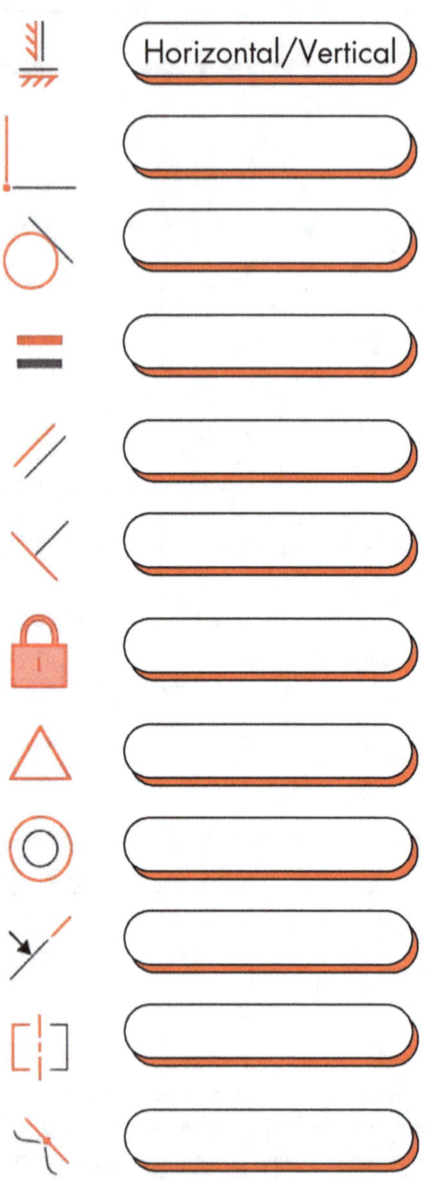

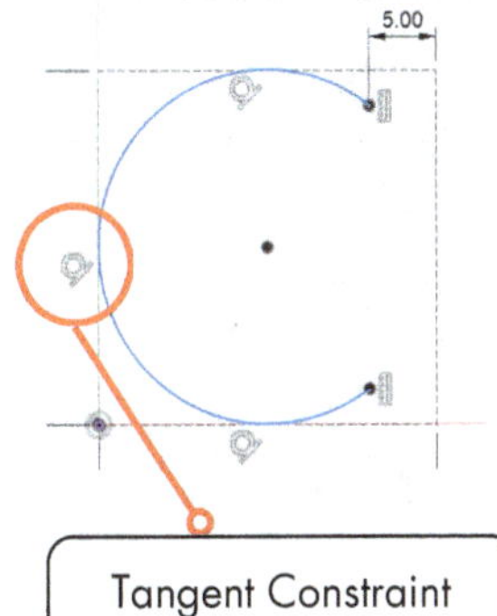

Using only Lines, Circles, Splines, and Arcs, sketch letters of the alphabet in a 25 x 25 mm box.

Type [R] and [X] to make a construction rectangle, click the Origin, move your cursor up and to the right, type 25, Tab, 25, and press Enter. Press [X] again to return to normal sketch geometry.

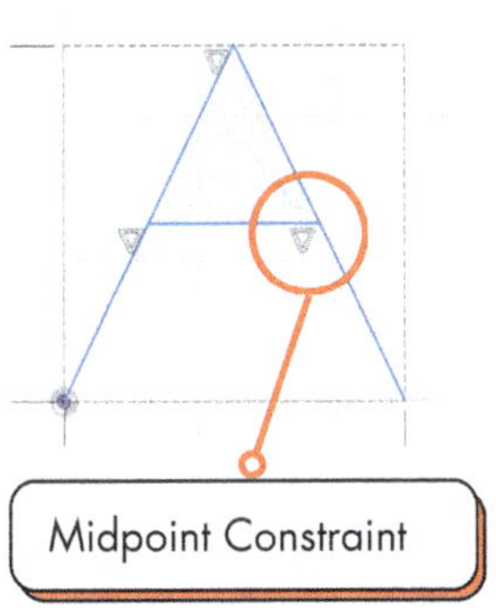

Try to make each letter using different constraints and geometry, or play with different fonts, serifs, and styles.

Notice 👀 that as you sketch, some symbols appear automatically. The software has automatically added a constraint.

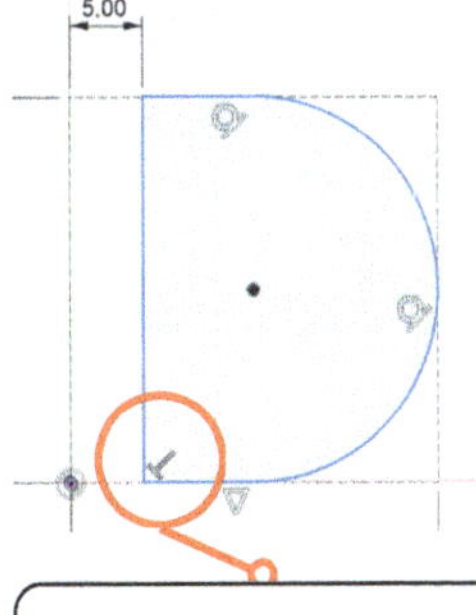

If you click on the symbol, it tells you what it is in the bottom left corner of the screen.

Hover over the corresponding button in the Sketch toolbar and it tells you what it is and what it does.

Post your challenge to our Discord community:

Intro: Saturn V Rocket 

Congratulations on mastering fundamental skills in Fusion! You've learned how to sketch, apply constraints and dimensions, add appearances, and use features like Extrude and revolve—all following the crucial 2D to 3D workflow.

Now it's time to apply these skills to recreate the iconic Saturn V Rocket which carried three Apollo astronauts to the moon and back.

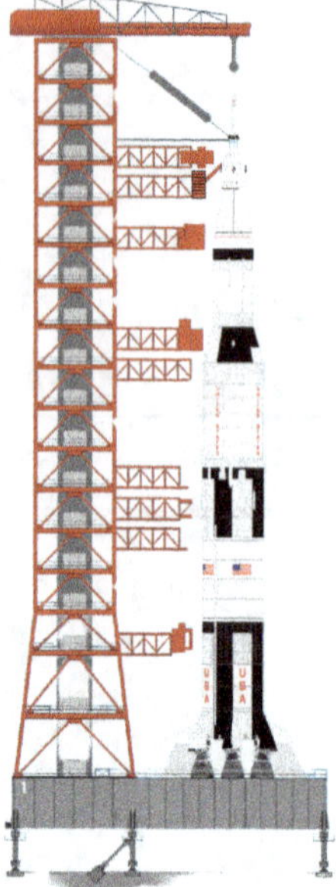

The Saturn V Rocket is a marvel of engineering. Key features include a classic cylindrical form tapering to a point, four powerful F-1 engines at its base generating nearly 7.7 million pounds of thrust, and a capsule designed to hold humans for weeks.

To recreate it you will stack tapered Extrusions, adding accurate appearances, then creating a thruster which you will duplicate using a new tool called Pattern. You will be creating a simplified version, so there is plenty of scope for you to dive in and add details, features, decals and much more.

Key learning:

- Constrain and dimension sketches
- Tapered Extrusions from faces
- Splitting faces
- Adding appearances to faces and bodies
- Pattern (circular) bodies
- Exporting for Augmented Reality (AR)

For a free and more detailed video walkthrough of this project, visit **CADclass.org** and sign up for a free trial for the Autodesk Fusion online course.

Saturn V Rocket 

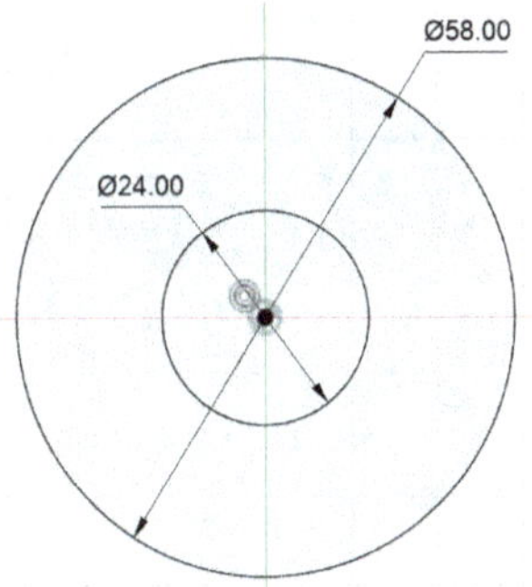

Create a new Sketch on the Top Plane and sketch a 24 mm and 58 mm circles [C] at the Origin. Finish the Sketch ✅.

Q? Were any constraints applied automatically? If so, which ones?

....

Get an Isometric view of your sketch and Extrude the ring profile upwards 365 mm. Open the Appearance tool and drag and drop White Paint onto the Body.

Q? Is there a way to make a shortcut to this appearance, e.g., "Add to Favorites"?

....

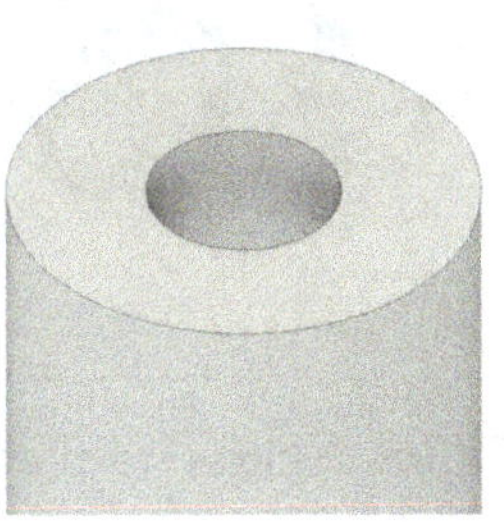

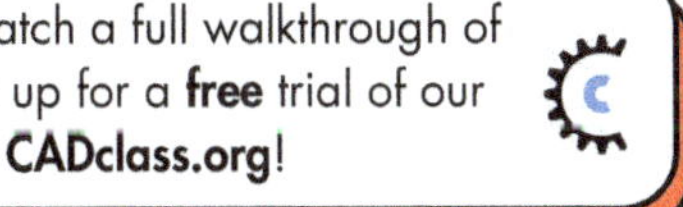

Create a New Sketch on the Extrusions top face, press [P] for Project, click on the ring profile, and click OK. This will allow you to Extrude both the ring profile and the inner circle at the same time. Finish the Sketch ✅ and get an isometric view.

Q? What would happen if you accidentally started your sketch on the top plane instead of the top face?

....

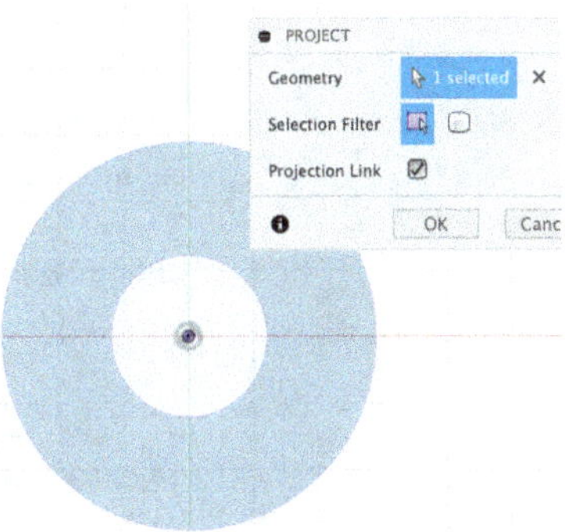

Saturn V Rocket 

Extrude the ring and the inner circular profiles up 32 mm, set the Taper Angle to -16 deg. Click OK

Q? What happens if you change the taper angle to +16 instead of -16?

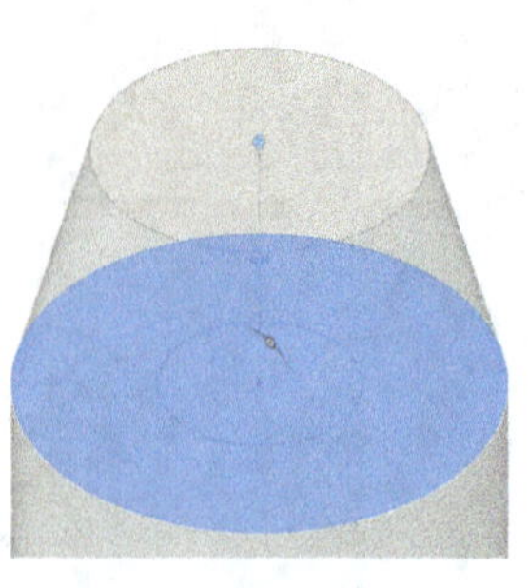

Search for Black Oxide in the Appearance tool, change the 'Apply To' to Faces and drag it onto the tapered cylindrical face.

Q? What is the difference between applying an Appearance to Bodies/Components vs Faces?

Extrude the top face of the Rocket body up 66 mm and click OK.

You can Extrude any flat face without making a new Sketch every time.

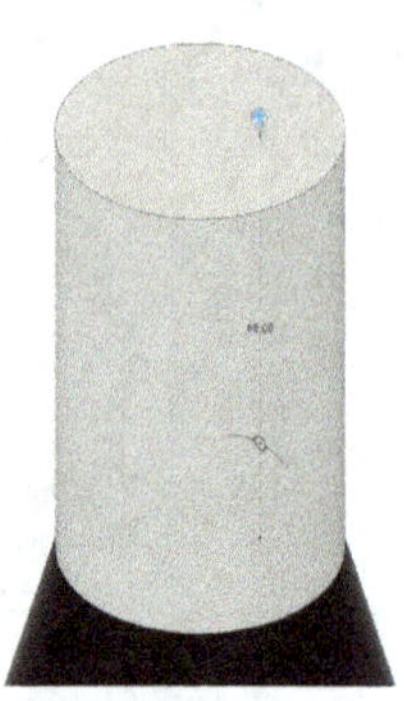

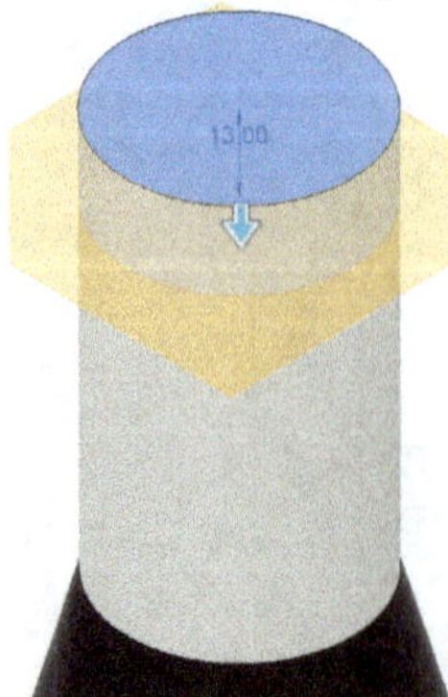

On the real Saturn V Rocket, this cylinder has a black ring at the top, so you need to use the Split Face tool to cut the face into a top and bottom.

Navigate to Construct >> Offset Plane, select the top face, set the Distance to -13 mm, and click OK.

Q? Why not just Extrude 2 cylinders on top of each other? What's different about splitting a face?

Saturn V Rocket 

Navigate to Modify >> Split Face. Select the top face, click 'Select' next to Splitting Tool, select the Offset Plane, and click OK.

Click the eye icon next to Construction in the Browser to hide the Offset Plane.

Open the Appearance tool, set 'Apply To' to Faces, and drag the Black Oxide appearance onto the top face.

Q? What is the bottom-most apperance in the available apperances (open all the sub-menus!)?

....

Repeat previous steps to Extrude the following set of cylinders and tapered cylinders:

Extrusion 4:   57 mm, -9 deg
Extrusion 5:   23 mm
Extrusion 6:   7 mm, -35.7 deg
Extrusion 7:   15 mm, -6 deg
Extrusion 8:   3 mm, -30 deg
Extrusion 9:   27 mm
Extrusion 10: 5 mm, -25 deg

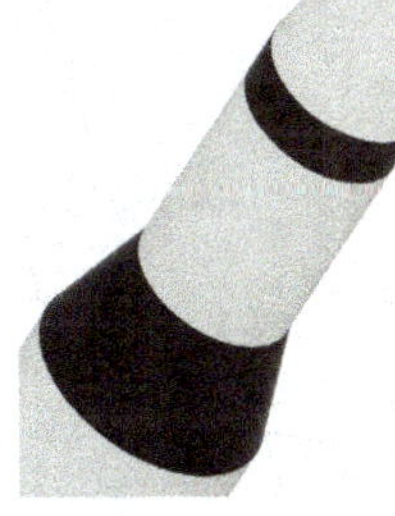

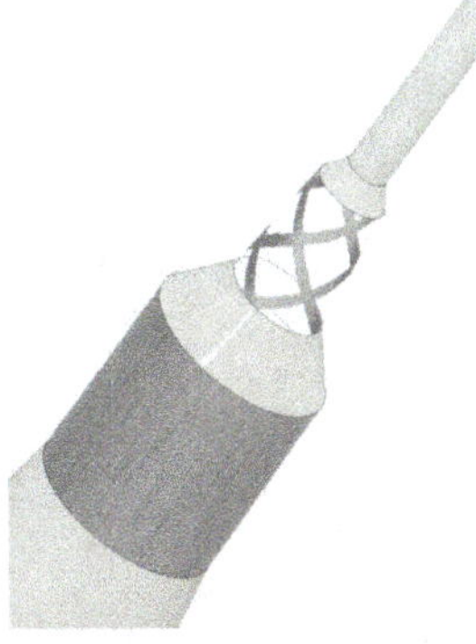

Open the Appearance tool, search for "Stainless Steel Brushed Linear Long", and apply it to Extrusion 5's cylindrical face.

Search for "Stainless Steel Mesh - Square Mesh", and apply it to Extrusion #7.

Then double click its icon and change the Rotation to 45 deg.

Saturn V Rocket 

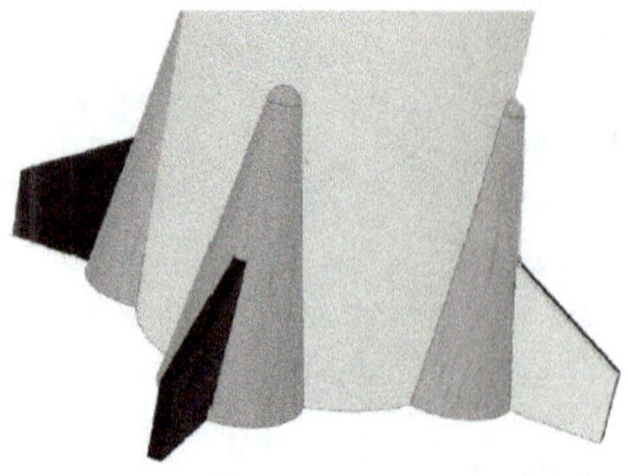

Since the 4 thrusters and fins are equally spaced, you can create 1 and then use the Circular Pattern tool to make the rest.

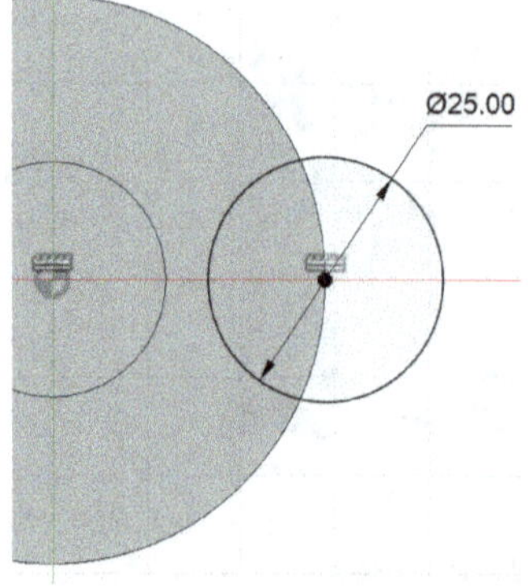

Orbit to the underside of the rocket and Create a new Sketch on the Rocket's bottom face.

Add a 25 mm circle near the X-axis, Horizontally constrain the circle's center to the Origin, and add a Coincident constraint to the circle's center and the outer circle's diameter.

Finish the Sketch ✅.

To verify if any of your sketches are fully Defined, expand Sketches in the Browser and check for a red padlock icon.

 Sketch1

 Sketch2

If there is a pencil icon, the sketch is Undefined.

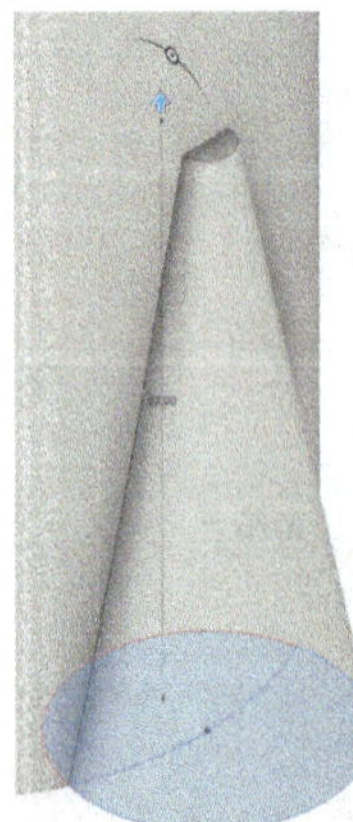

Type [E] for Extrude, select the 2 profiles that make up the circle, click the house icon on the ViewCube, and click and drag the blue arrow upwards -52 mm.

Set the Taper Angle to -11 deg and change the Operation from Cut to Join.

Q? What would happen if you accidentally set the operation to Cut?

....

Saturn V Rocket 

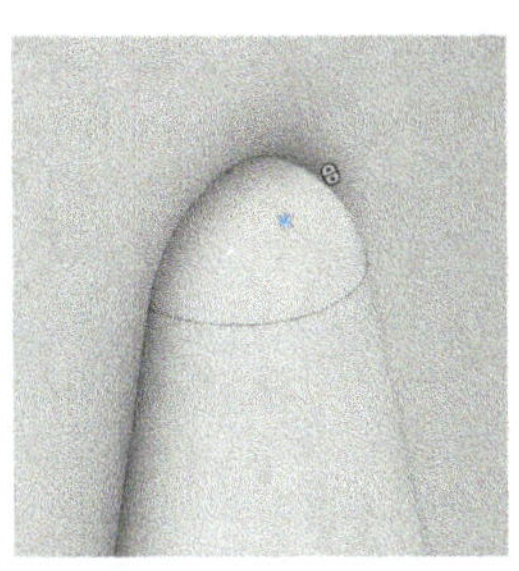

Press [F] for Fillet and select the tapered cylinder's top edge (not face). Set the Fillet size to 2.9 mm

Create a new Sketch on the Front Plane, sketch four lines, and make the bottom horizontal line to Coincident with the Origin.

Add the dimensions shown and verify the area inside the profile is light blue. Finish the Sketch ✓.

Q? Can you Extrude profiles that aren't light blue?

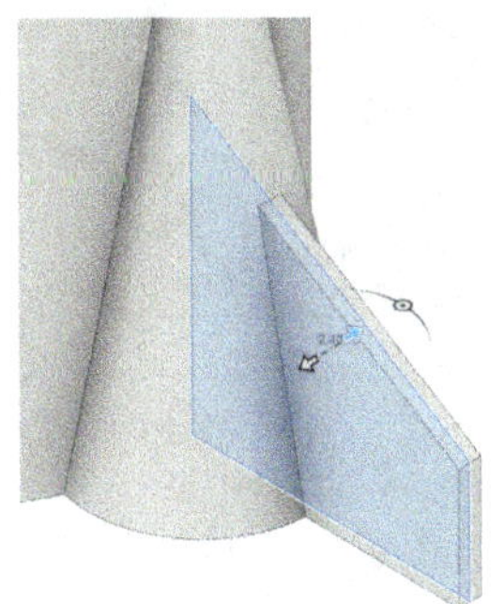

Extrude the profile, set the Direction to Symmetric, and change Measurement from Half Length to Whole Length. Set the Distance to 2.4 mm, and set the Operation to Join.

Q? Where else can you Start an Extrude?

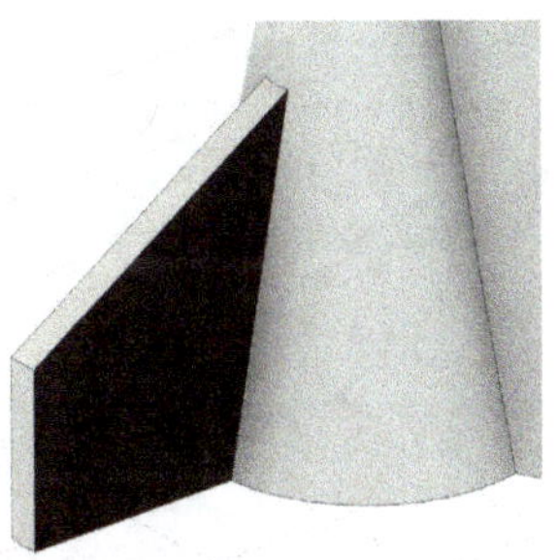

Orbit to the fin's other side and add the Black Oxide appearance.

Fun fact: On the real Saturn V Rocket, these colors were used to track the rocket's rotation.

Navigate to Create >> Pattern >> Circular Pattern, change the Object Type to Features, and select the two most recent Extrusions and the Fillet in the Timeline.

Click 'Select' next to Axis and select either the vertical blue Z-axis or the outer round surface. Increase the Quantity to 4 and click OK. Save your file 💾 .

Q? What other object types can you pattern?

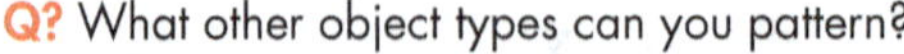

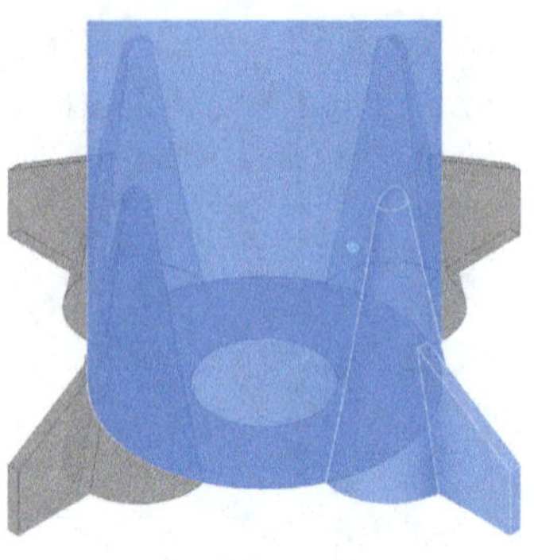

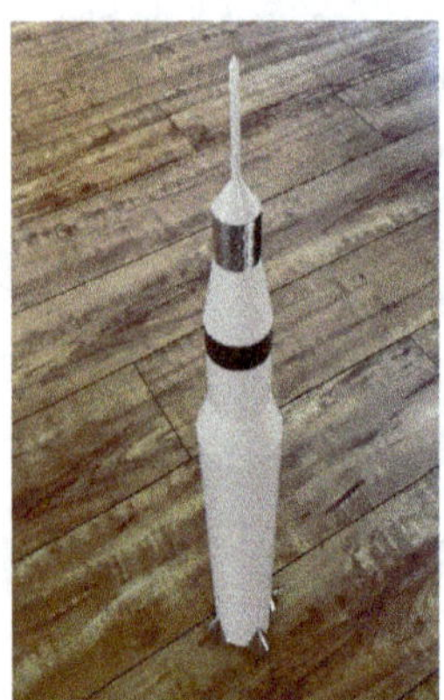

To view your rocket in AR (Augmented reality), navigate to File >> Export, and change the file type to .USDZ.

If you have an iPhone, upload the file to your Files app, open the Saturn V Rocket file, and point your camera at your tabletop.

If you use Android you may need to open your file on an AR viewer app like XR Viewer.

Review:

- To create the Rocket you stacked normal and tapered Extrusions
- To create the thrusters and fins, you created a new Extrusion and patterned it
- Notice again the 2D to 3D workflow

Reinforce & Stretch

Re-do the Rocket exercise from scratch with these variations:

- Make the Rocket have 6 thrusters, not 4.
- Double the scale of all dimensions e.g. 58 mm and 24 mm become 116 mm and 44 mm.

Explore these questions and try the prompts to find out what's possible:

1 - Is there a maximum distance you can Extrude to?

2 - What does the curved arc with the grey circle do that appears when Extruding?

3 - What does PressPull do when you select it and move a face?

4 - What appearance is bottom-most in the list?

5 - With Extrude activated, click and move the blue arrow below the face it joins. what does it do?

6 - What happens when you click the little black "i" in the Extrude dialogue box (bottom left corner)?

7. Which new terms can you fill out in the glossary in the back of the book?

Sketch a storyboard of how you would design, constrain, and dimension a tiered wedding cake.

Tool Review: Pattern

Pattern is a powerful tool for creating multiple copies of Sketches, Features, Bodies, or Components in a structured arrangement. It saves time and ensures consistency. You'll focus on Sketch and Feature Patterns now, but there are more.

Rectangular Patterns create copies in a grid-like arrangement.

Rectangular Patterns require several pieces of information: the object(s) to pattern, the direction, the spacing between or total span, and the quantity of objects.

The Dialog Box can be intimidating at first but you will find it gets easier after making a simple chess board grid of 25 x 25 mm squares in an 8 x 8 grid.

Note that the axes you pattern along don't need to be the X, Y and Z axes, but can be any lines.

Circular patterns require 3 inputs:

1 - what objects are being patterned
2 - about what axis, and
3 - the quantity.

The Objects can be changed based on selection as entire Bodies, Features that make up parts of a Body, or even individual Faces that make up a Feature.

The Axis can be the X, Y, or Z axis, a line in a sketch, or any cylindrical face or edge that shares the same axis that you want your objects to be patterned around.

Circular patterns create copies in a radial arrangement around an axis.

True or False?

Q: Extrude can only be used to add material, not to remove it.

Q: You can Extrude directly from a flat face without creating a new Sketch every time.

Q: When using the Extrude tool you can specify a taper angle to create angled surfaces.

Q: You can apply appearances to individual faces as well as bodies or components.

Q: You can use the "Project" tool to create Sketch geometry based on existing 3D features.

Review

Toggle Show/Hide icon — [?]

Isometric view icon — [?]

[?] — Finish Sketch icon

[?] — Extrude

Circle — [?]

[?] — A

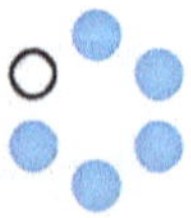

Challenge 1:

If you feel energized by this, consider using other tools inside of Fusion to customize your Rocket and make it look better.

Experiment with the Appearance, Decal, and Emboss tool.

Challenge 2:

Sketch the form of a fidget spinner here:

Now try it in Fusion…

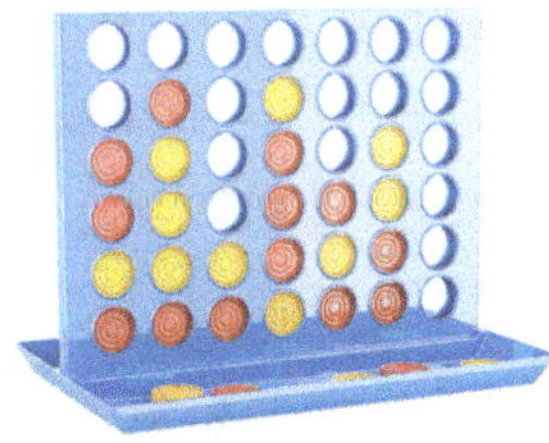

Sketch the form of a 4-in-a-row game here:

Then try it in Fusion…

Post your challenge to our Discord community:

Storyboard the sketches, features, and tools used to create this (use some, or all of these boxes, as necessary).

2D > 3D

Storyboard the sketches, features, and tools that could be used to recreate this toy brick with an open bottom (use some, or all of these boxes, as necessary).

Design Intent

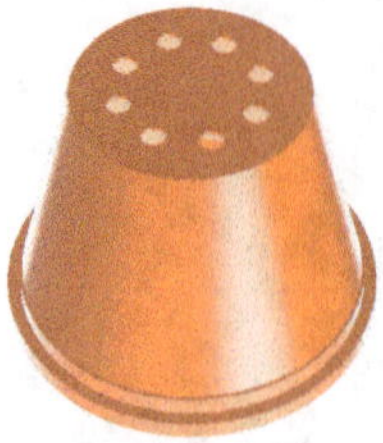

1. 2D Sketch (Profile)
2. Constrain & Dimension
3. Revolve (New Body)
4. Shell
5. 2D Sketch (1 x Hole)
6. Circular Pattern
7. Extrude (Cut)

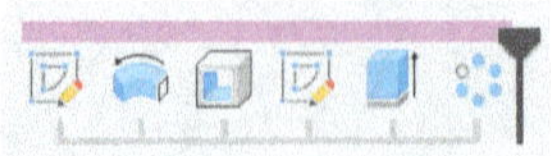

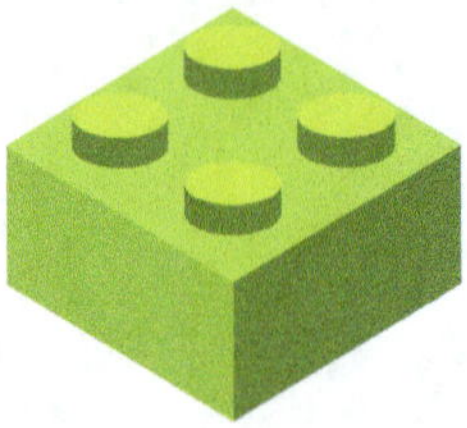

1. 2D Sketch (Profile)
2. Constrain & Dimension
3. Extrude (New Body)
4. 2D Sketch (1 x Stud)
5. Extrude (Join)
6. Rectangular Pattern
7. Shell

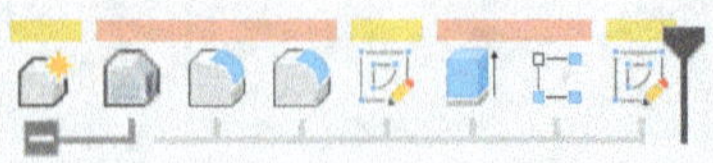

Now that you've explored several methods for creating 3D objects from 2D sketches, it's time to dive into another powerful tool: Sweep. The Sweep tool allows you to "drag" a 2D shape along a designated path. For example, sweeping two rails along an intricately curved path becomes a roller coaster track.

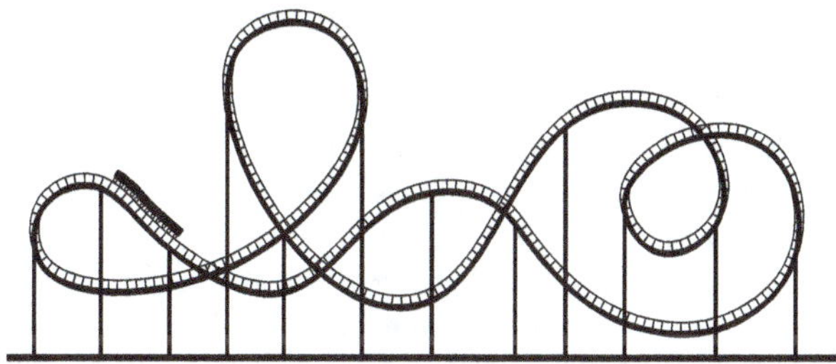

In this section, you'll design a 3D Printable Carabiner by sweeping a rectangular profile along a curved path, then refining the shape by rounding off or beveling sharp edges.

Once again, the core concept remains: 2D sketches to 3D objects. This time, however, you'll take it further by modifying your 3D object with a Chamfer (beveled edge), a Fillet (rounded edge), and a few Extrude-cuts to add flexibility to your 3D print.

The new workflow is 2D sketches become 3D objects and then 3D objects can be modified.

Key Skills:

- Sweep a profile along a path
- Modify a 3D object with the Modify tools
- Continue practicing the core skills of sketches, constraints, and dimensions

For a free and more detailed video walkthrough of this project, visit **CADclass.org** and sign up for a free trial for Autodesk Fusion.

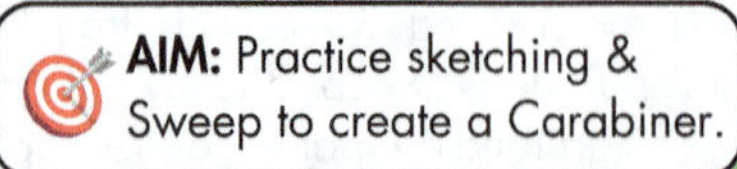

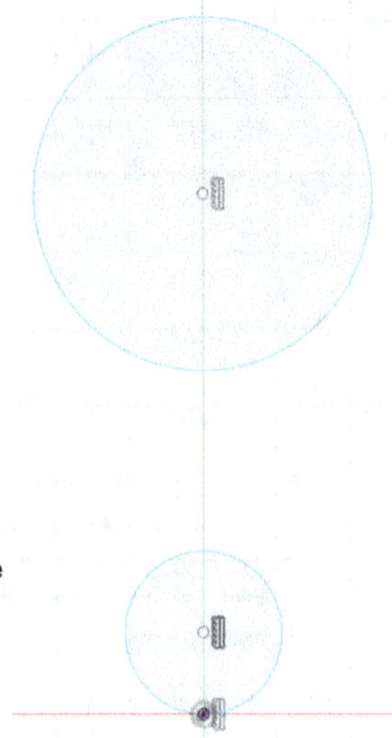

Save Carabiner to the Fusion Fundamentals folder.

Sketch two circles on the Y-Axis of the Top Plane.
Hold ctrl/cmd, Select both circles and the origin, and
apply a vertical constraint.

Select the Coincident constraint and click the lower
circle and the Origin, so the bottom point of the circle
passes through the Origin.

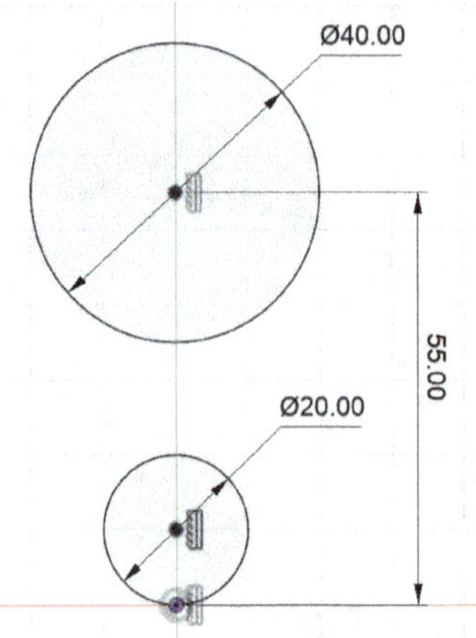

Add the Dimension shown.

Q? How do you know if your sketch is fully
defined?

....

If it is not, click and drag the undefined
geometry to see how it can move and add
dimensions or constraints to correct it.

[L] for Line, move your cursor to the center of
the top circle, move horizontally to the left,
click to place the first endpoint, and click on
the left side of the lower circle.

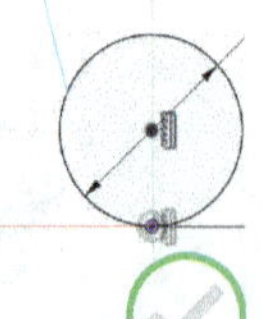

Notice the dashed blue line - - - and a blue X.
These are inferred constraints.

Q? Are inferred constraints always useful?

....

Repeat this step on the other side.

Add 4 Tangent constraints between the lines and circles as shown.

Q? Why might some tangent constraints already be applied? Did you need to apply all 4 or did you get a warning message?

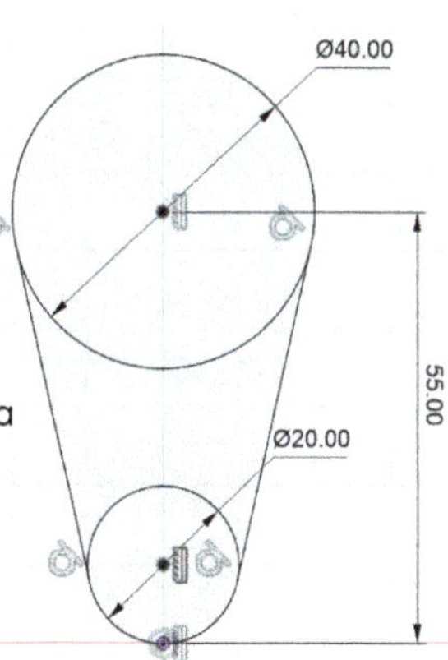

....

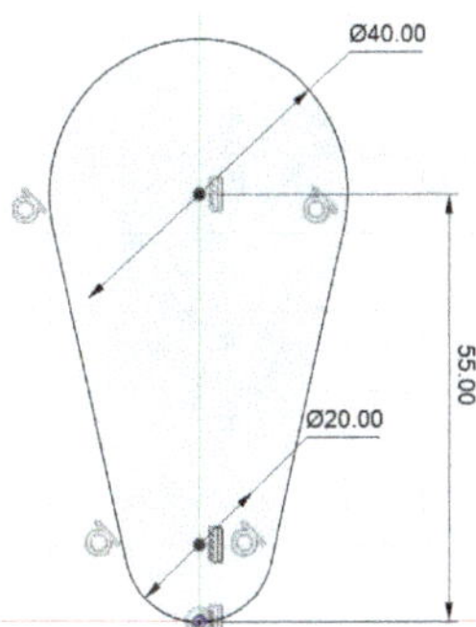

Trim [T] and remove the inner arc's of the circles to leave you with a single Carabiner shaped profile.

Any extra lines or arcs touching the Path will cause an error.

Finish the Sketch ✅ and get an Isometric view.

New Sketch on the Right Plane. Create and dimension a Center Point Rectangle from the origin. Finish the Sketch ✅.

Q? When you hover your mouse over the Center Point Rectangle button, do you see the three dots? Click them and write below about what they do:

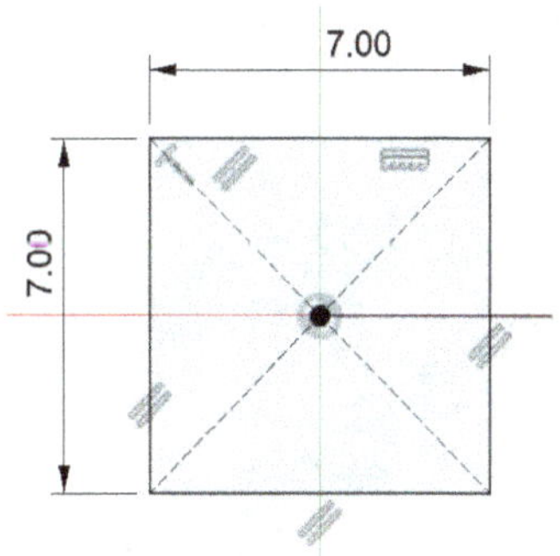

....

There are two ways to fully define this sketch that take the same amount of time.

1 - Dimension both lines to 7 mm.
2 - Dimension one side and use the Equal constraint.

Q? Which way do you think is "better" and why?

....

Carabiner 

Sweep creates 3D objects by moving a 2D profile along a 2D or 3D path.

Sweep requires two sketches: a **Profile** and a **Path**. 

Navigate to Create >> Sweep. Select the profile and path and click OK.

Q? Why is the profile pre-selected? ....

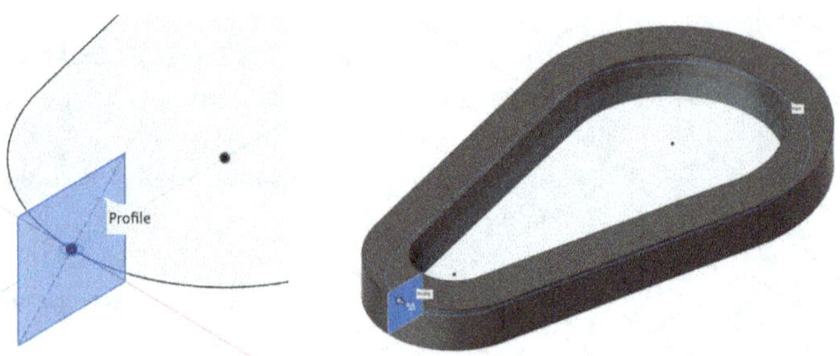

Q? What happens if you change the twist angle to 180?

....

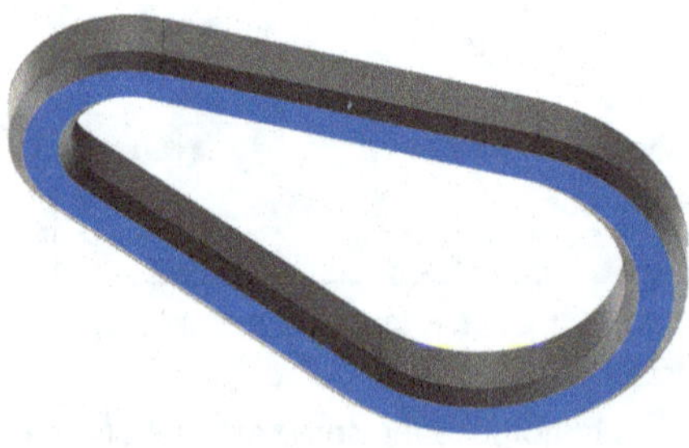

Modify >> Chamfer, select the bottom face, and set the Distance to 1.5 mm.

Q? What happens if you set it to 20 mm?

....

In manufacturing, sharp edges are almost always removed. Fillets (rounded) and chamfers (angled) are the most common techniques for removing them.

Because this Carabiner is designed to be 3D Printed, it is beneficial to Chamfer the underside of the part to prevent drooping and to Fillet the rest of the part.

New sketch on the Carabiner's top face.

Slot >> Center to Center Slot, click the Origin, move your cursor up and click on the Midpoint of the arc's edge. Click again and move your cursor sideways, type 1, and press Enter. Finish Sketch ✅.

Q? Could you have created the sketch on the top plane instead of the top face? What would have changed?

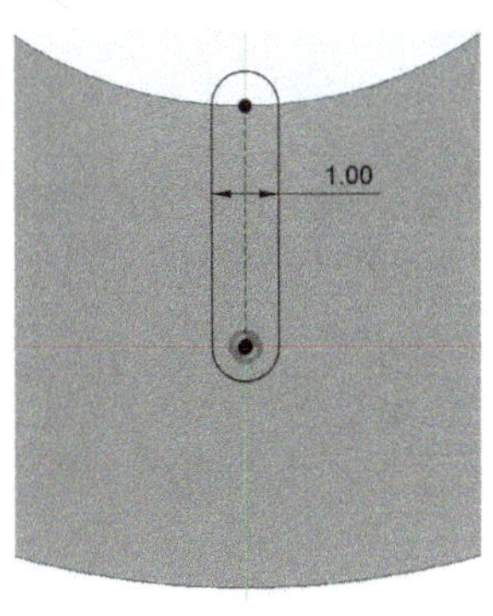

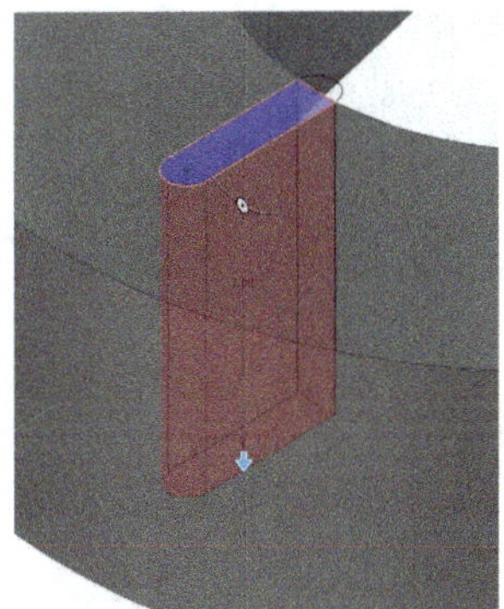

Click the Viewcube's House Icon for an isometric view. Extrude Cut the slot -7 mm.

Q? What happens if you set the Extent Type to All? Do you think that affects your design later?

New sketch on the Carabiners Top Face. Make the slots shown. Use the Equal and the Parallel constraints and add the following dimensions. Fully define the Sketch.

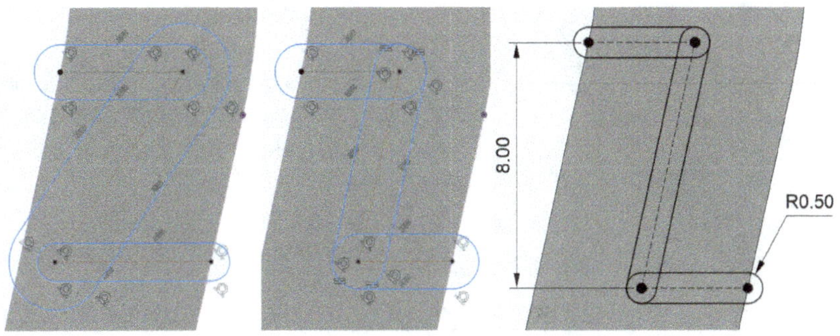

Finish the Sketch ✅.

Get an Isometric View, and Extrude cut through the Body.

Q? Did you use a dimension or Extent Type?

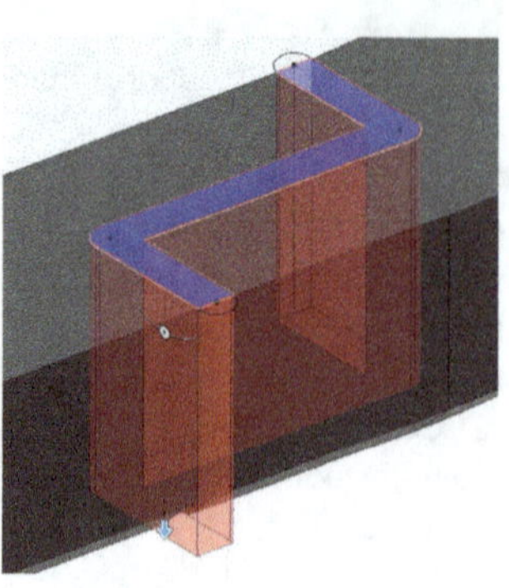

....

Add a 1 mm Fillet to the top face.

Uh oh... When you do this, you get an error message because of the sharp geometry.

Q? Is there a number that does not cause this error?

....

One way to fix this is to navigate to the Timeline and click and drag the History Marker (vertical black line) before the most recent Extrude feature.

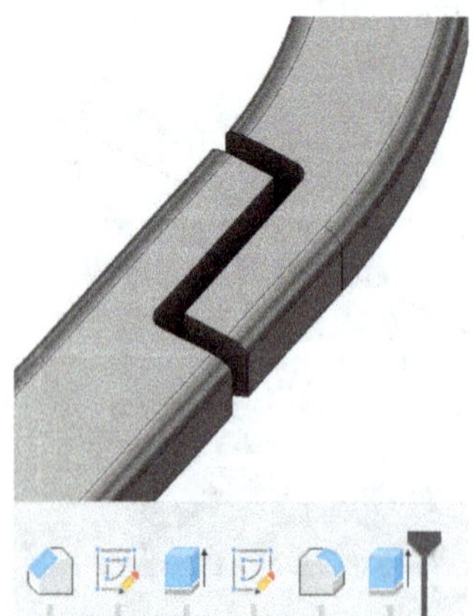

Open the Fillet tool again, select the top face, set the distance to 1mm, and click OK.

Then move the History Marker back to the right side (the present). This will include both the Fillet and the Extrude feature.

Q? What does this information say about how the timeline works?

....

Carabiner 

Parametric design in CAD means creating models in a chronological order of Features, e.g., Sketch 1, Extrude 1, Fillet 1. Features are generated in a specific order in the Timeline. Features on the Timeline can be edited and reordered to change how parts are generated. 📌

Change the appearance [A] of the carabiner to 3D printing filament you have on hand or to your favorite color.

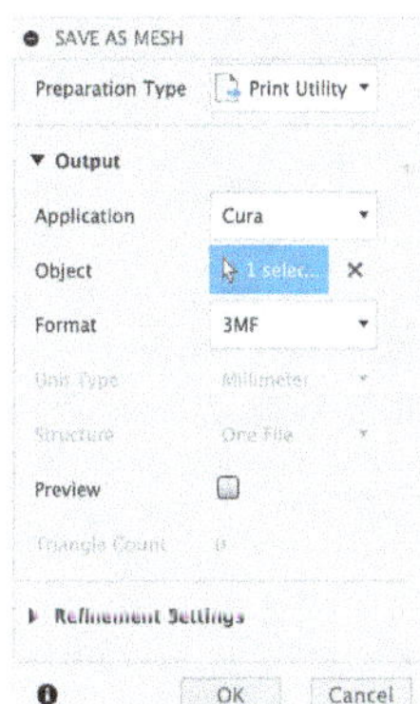

To save the file as an STL for 3D printing you can export it and change the filetype, or launch the file directly into your slicer from Fusion.

Expand Bodies in the Browser, right-click Body1, Save As Mesh, set the Preparation Type to Print Utility, and set the Application to your preferred Slicer. Now when you click OK it will open your slicer and load your file into it automatically!

For those new to 3D printing, slicing is the process of turning a 3D model into a 3D printable file.

Review:
- To create the Carabiner you Swept a Profile around a Path
- You Extrude-cut to make a latch and also modified the Body with a Chamfer and Fillet
- Notice the 2D to 3D to Modify workflow

Edit every stage in the timeline of the completed Carabiner and make variations.

Explore these questions and try the prompts to find out what's possible:

1. Change the diameters of the starting circles and the distance between them.

2. Make the profile square MUCH bigger.

3. Right-click >> rename to rename all the Sketch and Extrude features to something logical.

4. Drag and move the Timeline features to scramble them.

5. Can you rearrange them, or do you have to use Undo?

6. As you move them, do any of the constraints stop you?

7. Can the profile be too big for the path?

8. Did you notice some features were hidden (grey eye) in the browser list? Did you do that?

9. What happened when you moved a feature that didn't have the necessary information from the previous feature e.g. an Extrude without a Sketch?

10. Which new terms can you fill out in the glossary in the back of the book?

Try to recreate a classic paperclip using as few steps as possible. Play with the (somewhat tricky) feature to create an arc from the endpoint of a line: Click and drag the endpoint of a line to create a tangent arc.

Tool Review: Sweep

Sweep creates 3D objects by tracing a 2D profile along a 2D path. It works by following the path's direction, adding complexity to shapes. You can control the profile, path, and even twist angles for more advanced designs.

A sweep profile can be joined back up with itself or be disconnected. The carabiner joins back up with itself but the spring shown here does not.

The spring is a circle swept along a helix and is left "open".

Unlike the other Create tools, the distance the Profile is swept is not a dimension, but a fraction of the length of the Path. If the Body is half the length of the Path, then the Distance would be set to 0.5 = 50%.

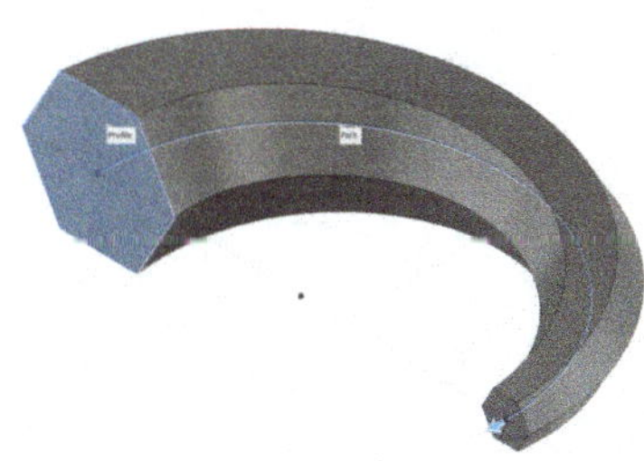

If your Path is disconnected, you can also take advantage of the Taper Angle which reduces the size of your profile along the Path.

This makes it easy to model an animal's or instrument's horn.

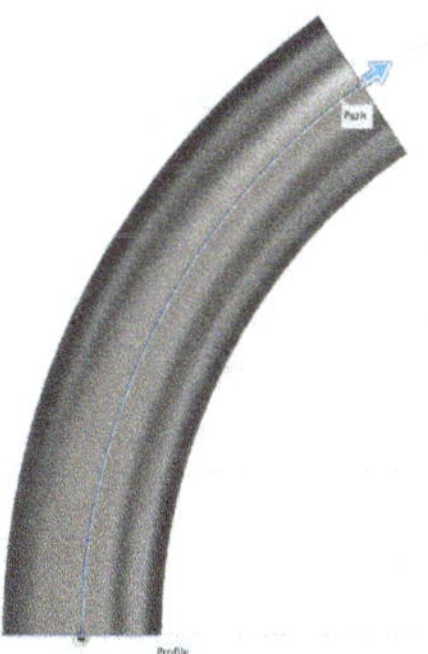

You can also change the Orientation of the Profile to follow Perpendicularly along the Path or to remain parallel to the original Profile.

Try it and see what happens…

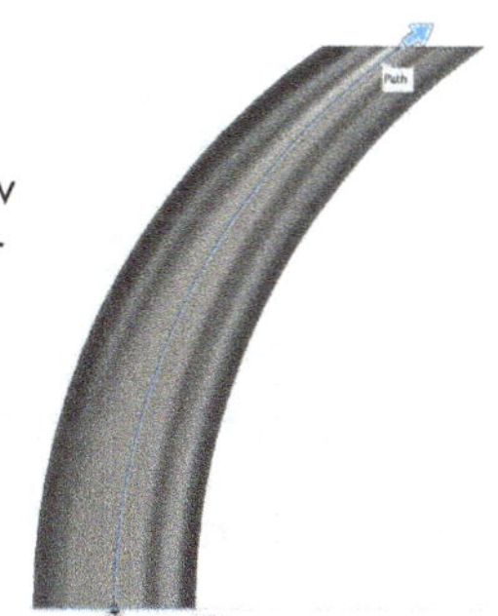

True or False?

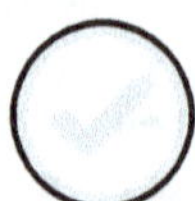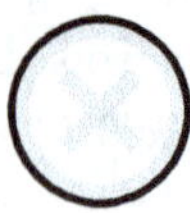

Q: A Sweep operation requires only one Sketch to create a 3D object.

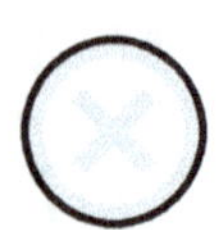

Q: You can create your own shortcut keys.

Q: The "Twist Angle" in the Sweep feature can only be set to 180 degrees.

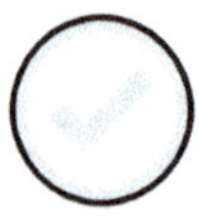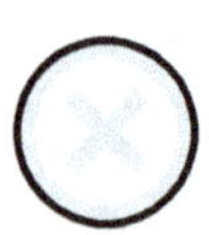

Q: A Fillet applies a radius to an edge, while a Chamfer applies a 45 deg bevel.

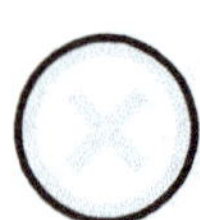

Q: The Timeline allows users to reorder Features to change the order that parts are generated.

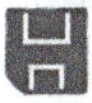

Line

T

Apperance

Sweep icon

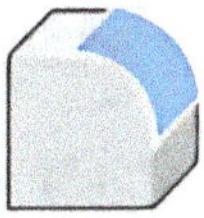

Challenge 1:

Make a Swept text nameplate. Add some text to the Top plane, an arc to the Right plane, sweep the text, and join a baseplate to the bottom face of the text.

Challenge 2:

Combine everything you have learned about Sweeping and Extruding and design a set of 3 Allen Keys and a plastic holder.

You can make all 3 Paths, all 3 Profiles, and the Holder profile in 2 Sketches.

Add appearances and Physical Materials to make your project look as realistic and functional as possible.

Post your challenge to our Discord community:

Intro: Finger Surfboard 

Imagine standing at the beach, looking out over the vast ocean. The waves are powerful yet fluid, and surfers move through them with ease. Before those surfers ever ride them, their surfboards start as 2D designs, flat outlines on paper or screen. But much like how the ocean shapes the waves, CAD modeling breathes life into those designs, transforming them from drawings into 3D forms and eventually, boards ready to ride.

In this chapter, you'll explore how to take multiple flat 2D profiles of a surfboard and sculpt it into a fully realized 3D object using the Loft tool. You'll begin with sketches—outlining the length, width, and board's curvature. From there, you'll shape the size, curvature and fin placement, translating ideas into something you can imagine riding. By the end, you'll see how moving from 2D to 3D is more than a technical step—it's where design starts to feel real, and your surfboard goes from lines on a screen to a creation capable of slicing through the waves.

Key Skills:

- Sketching on multiple parallel Offset planes
- Lofting between profiles and points
- Ellipse Sketch tool

For a free and more detailed video walkthrough of this project, visit **CADclass.org** and sign up for a free trial for Autodesk Fusion.

Finger Surfboard

In this project, you'll make 4 Offset Planes from the Right plane and 4 separate sketches on those planes.

Navigate to Construct, and make an Offset Plane 24 mm from the Right Plane. Click OK.

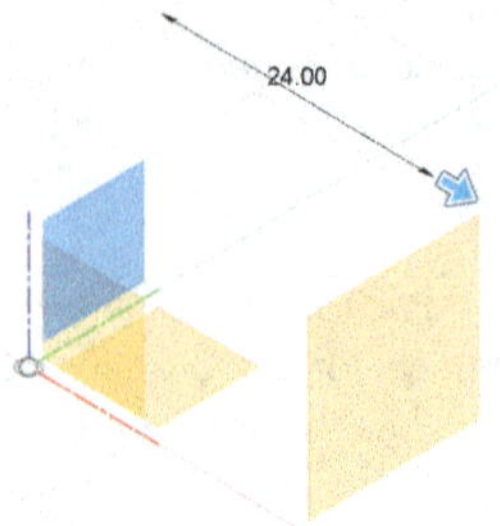

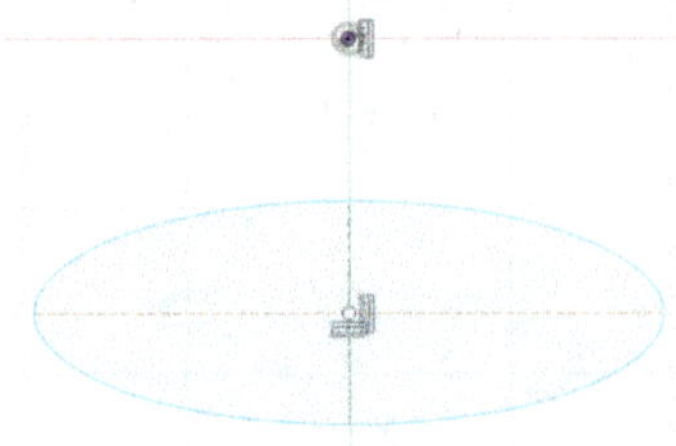

Create a new Sketch on this plane and add an Ellipse below the Origin and Vertically constrain its center to the Origin.

Dimension the ellipse's width, height, and distance from the origin as shown.

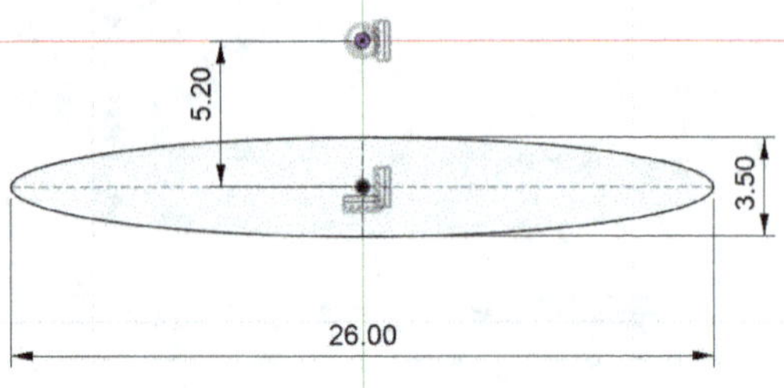

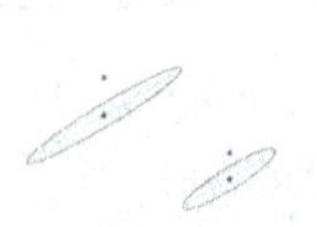

Repeat this process 3 times:

1. Construct an Offset Plane from the Right Plane.
2. Make a new Sketch on this Plane.
3. Draw an ellipse below the Origin, Vertically Constrain it, and add the height, width, and center to the Origin dimensions.
4. (See next page for specifics).

Finger Surfboard 

Ellipse #	Plane Offset Distance	Ellipse Width	Ellipse Height	Ellipse Center-to-Origin
2	72 mm	38.0 mm	4.0 mm	7.0 mm
3	116 mm	29.6 mm	4.0 mm	6.0 mm
4	140 mm	18.0 mm	4.0 mm	4.2 mm

Navigate to Create >> Loft, click the ellipses in Sketch 4, 3, 2, 1, and then the Workspace Origin in that order.

The Surfboard shape will appear as you go.

Q? What other Operations other than New Body are available in Loft?

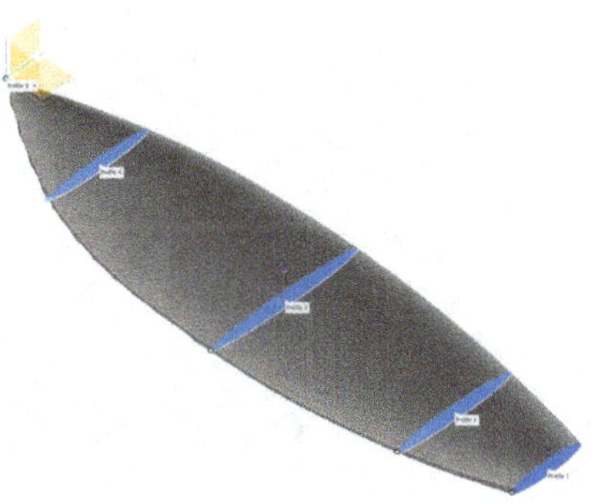

....

Add a Polystyrene appearance and change the scale to 42%.

Zoom in and notice the color has changed and that there's a new bubbly foam decal.

Finish the Sketch ✅.

Create a new Sketch on the Front Plane.

Draw and connect the fin by Projecting [P] the geometry and then drawing a spline and a line that joins its endpoints.

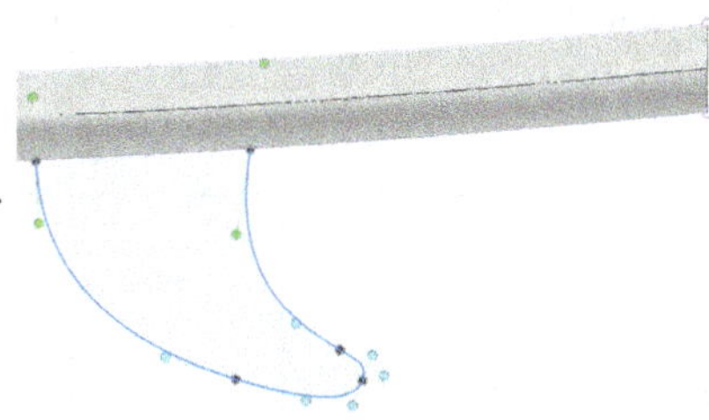

Q? How else could you draw a fin?

....

Finger Surfboard 

Finish the Sketch ✅ and Symmetrically Extrude the profile until it looks right. Set the Operation to Join and click OK.

If the fin is a different color to the board, edit the Extrude feature and change the Operation from New Body to Join.

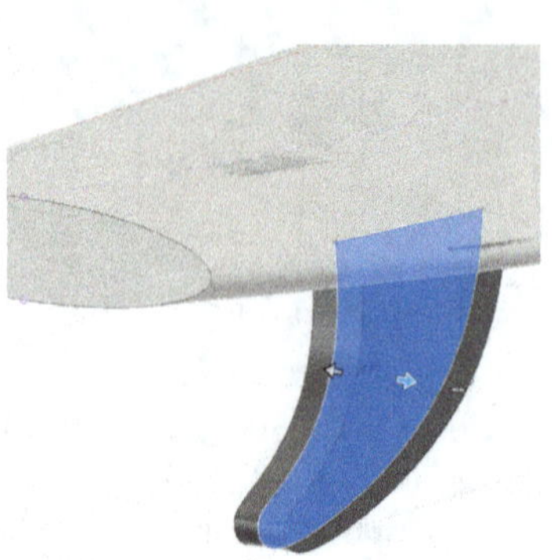

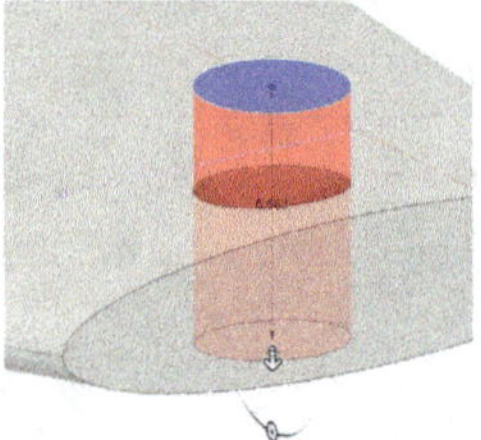

Create a new Sketch on the Top plane. Draw, Dimension, Constrain, Finish the Sketch ✅, and Extrude-Cut a 4 mm circle through the board.

Q? What's the name of another tool you could use to do the same thing?

....

Save your file 💾 as "Finger Surfboard", and export it as an STL to be 3D Printed.

Thread some string through the hole, tie a knot, and tie another end around your ring finger. Have a friend get up to speed, lower your window, and ride your surfboard in the air!

Q? Ask the Autodesk Assistant (in the bottom right corner): "Are there other ways to save an STL file?"What does it suggest?

....

With all these planes and sketches, the browser can become confusing. Try to right-click on Features in the Timeline and rename them logically and methodically, e.g., Offset Plane 1 (smallest ellipse).

Explore these questions and try the prompts to find out what's possible:

1 - Change the order of the profiles to click on, does the order matter?

2 - Is there maximum size ellipse that "breaks" the loft tool?

3 - Can a Loft do a "cut" like you can in Extrude?

4 - What do you think the "rails" option in the dialogue box means?

5 - As you Loft, the 3D shape 'grows" as you click

6 - Can entire profiles be mirrored?

7 - Does the Pattern tool help reduce repetition?

8 - What happenes if you re-order features in the Timeline?

9. Which new terms can you fill out in the glossary in the back of the book?

Sketch a storyboard of how you would design, constrain, and dimension the profiles and planes to recreate a hockey stick and puck

Loft creates 3D shapes by smoothly joining 2 (or more) 2D profiles or cross-sections. These profiles are usually separated on parallel Offset Planes. Loft is commonly used to create complex curved surfaces or objects with varying cross-sections.

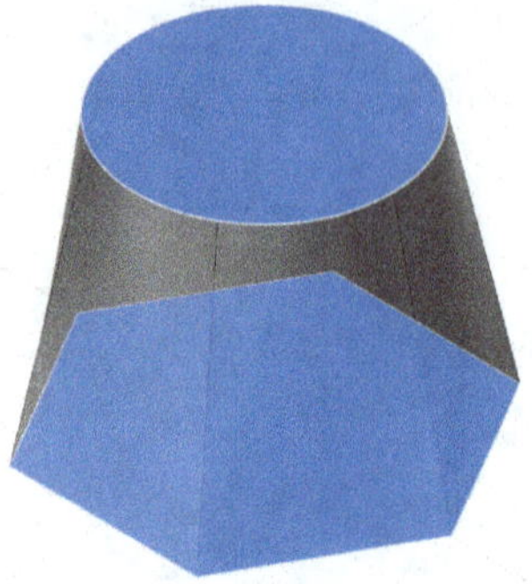

Lofting can create complicated 3D objects from simple sketches and is especially useful for making real-world connectors between any two objects (Think dust-collection port and vacuum). These 3D objects can be made by joining 2 or more profiles, points, or a combination of both.

The planes that the profiles are sketched on, don't need to be parallel. You can make a series of Sketches on Planes "Along a Path".

When you Loft and still have the Dialog Box open, you will see white dots on every corner or vertex of each profiles.

You can click and drag these points around the profiles to add more faces to the Body and create twisted and more intricate features.

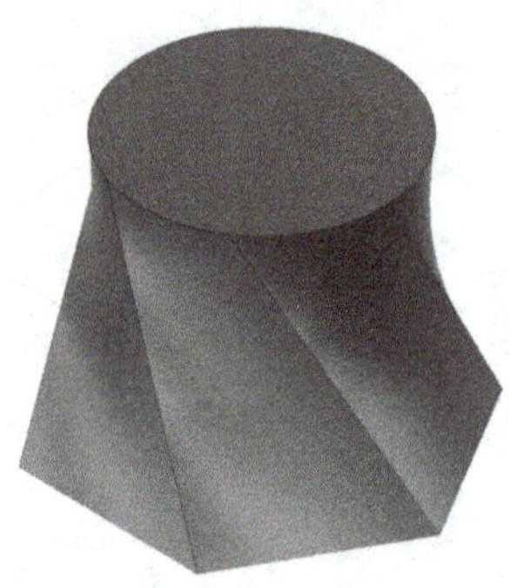

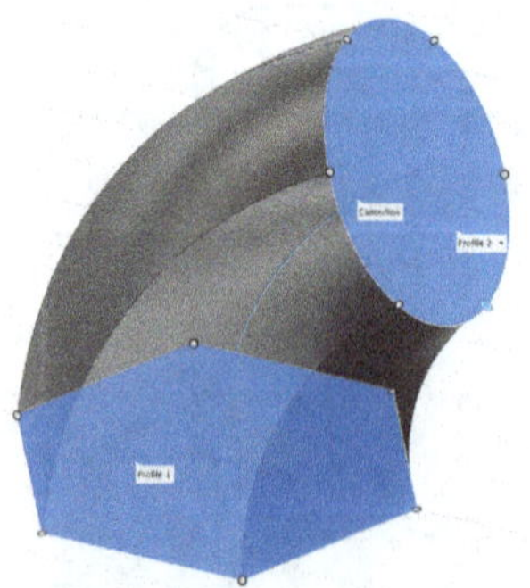

The examples above are Lofting which joins two profiles along the shortest distance, a straight line. But you can also use Rails, curved or straight lines that act as guides for lofting to move along, similar to the Sweep tool.

Here you can see a hexagon Lofting to a circle along an Arc.

Play around and see what whacky designs you can make! It gets interesting...

True or False?

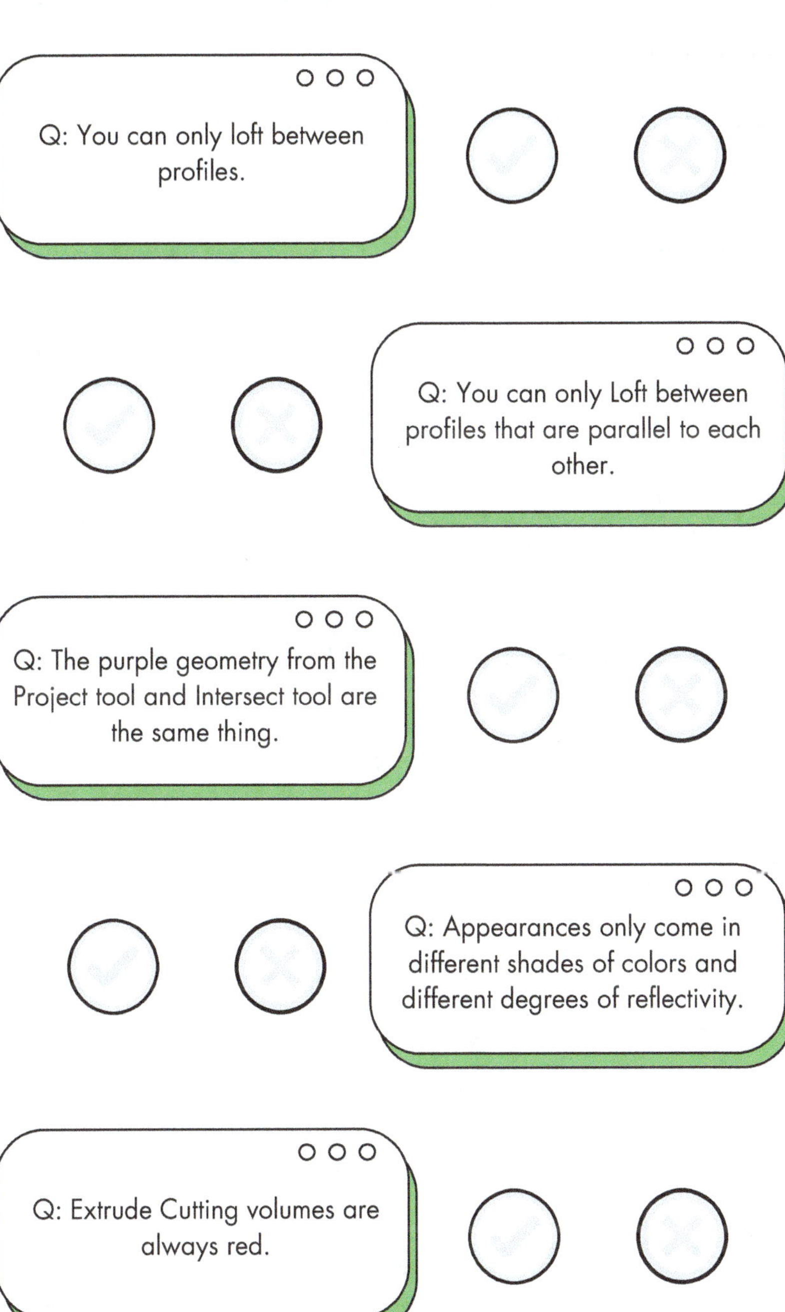

E

P

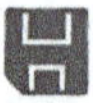

Circle

Fit Point is a type of...

Apperance

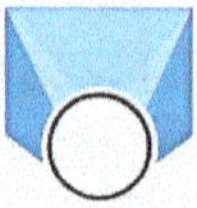

Ellipse

Challenge

Challenge 1:

Use the Loft tool and Offset Planes to make a glass bottle with a distinct and curvy profile.

Find a reference image as a guide to make shapes on Offset Planes parallel to the Top Plane.

Challenge 2:

Using several profiles, along a curved path, make either an instrument's or an animal's horn.

Each Profile can be made on a Plane along the path using the tool Plane Along Path in the Construct menu.

Bonus points for appearances and textures.

Post your challenge to our Discord community:

Intro: Pizza Cutter 

It's time to take your CAD skills to the next level by designing a practical, real-world object—a pizza cutter. This project will introduce you to the power of Joints and assemblies in CAD. Instead of creating individual bodies, you'll make components that come together, move, and interact in a functional design.

To create the pizza cutter you'll make three Components: the handle, the blade, and the pin connecting the handle and the blade. You'll model each part separately using Components, then add Joints, and then motion. By the end, you'll have a pizza cutter with a spinning blade.

Assemblies unlock your ability as a CAD designer to take your skills to the next level!

Key Skills:

- How to assemble multiple components
- How to use and animate Joints to make realistic movements

All assembly projects that require moving parts must be made from Components (not Bodies) and connected with Joints. Joints allow for linear and rotational movement, a combination of both, or no movement at all.

Pizza Cutter

AIM: Create, assemble and join parts of a pizza cutter.

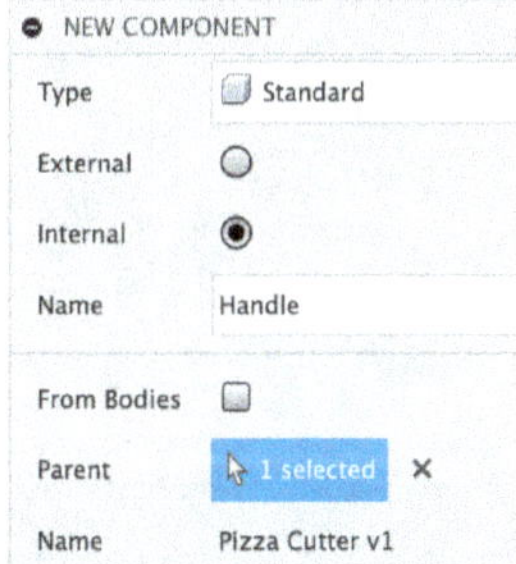

Save your file 💾 as "Pizza Cutter" and navigate to Assemble >> New Component.

Verify Internal is checked, name the part Handle and click OK.

This is how you will start every Component. 📌

New Sketch on the Front Plane, Center to Center Slot, Coincident constraint between the slot's centerline and the Origin, and add the following dimensions.

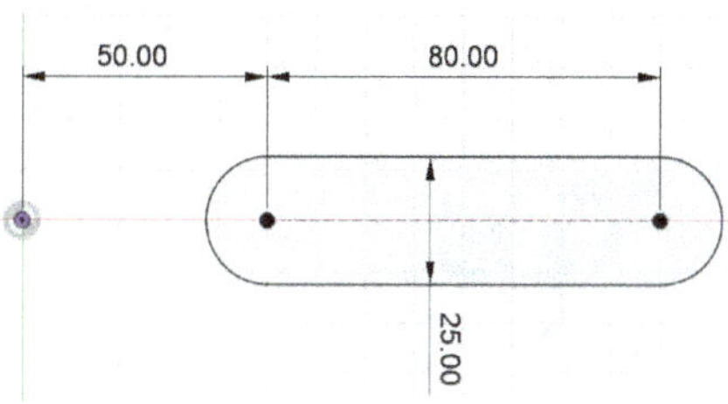

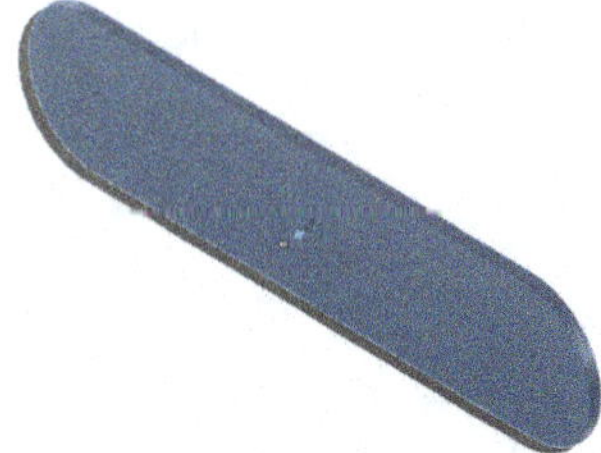

Finish the Sketch ✅.

Extrude the profile -2 mm.

New Sketch on the front face.

Center to Center slot from the Origin to the right center of the previous slot. Add a 5 mm circle at the Origin. Add the dimensions shown. Finish Sketch ✅.

Pizza Cutter

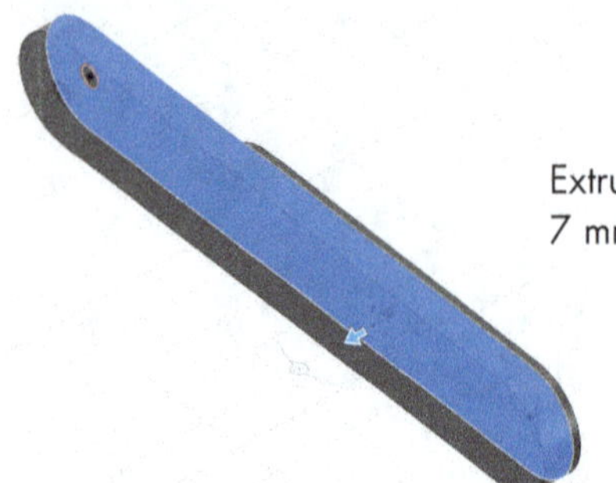

Extrude the two profiles that make up the slot 7 mm, but not the circle.

New Sketch, Rectangle, front face. Coincident with top and bottom edges.

Add dimensions and Finish the Sketch ✅.

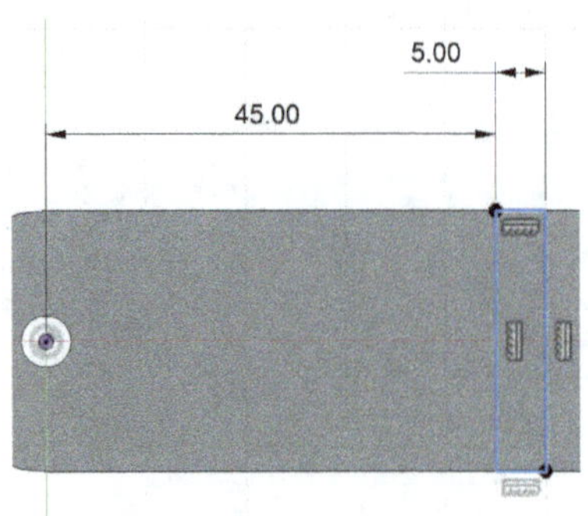

Extrude this rectangular profile 15 mm out.

Fillet the front vertical edges 2.5 mm as shown below so the front face is domed.

Mirror the Body about the Front Plane, highlight the entire Body and add a 1.5 mm Fillet.

Add a wooden appearance (this is oak)

Edit the settings to look more like real wood

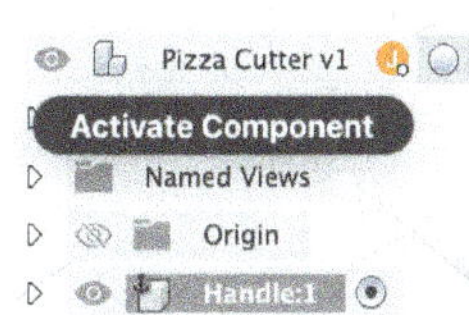

This component is all done! Hover your cursor over the Pizza Cutter text at the top of the Browser (the Root Component). Click the gray dot to the right of it to Activate it.

Q? What happens if you forget to do that?

....

Assemble >> New Component, name it "Pin" and verify it is set to Internal.

This pin will pass through the hole in the handle holding the blade in place while allowing it to rotate.

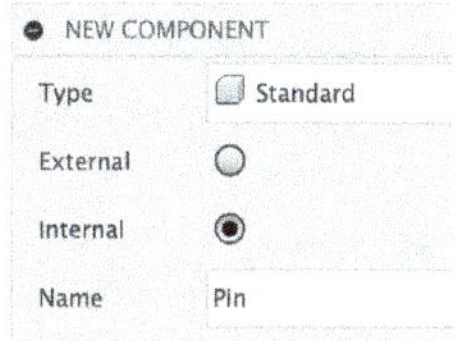

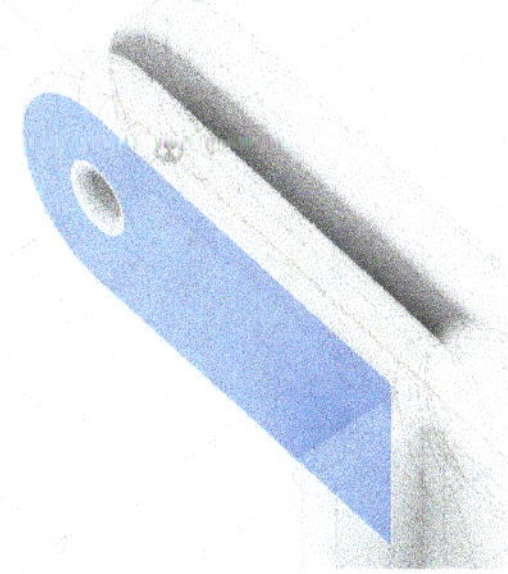

New Sketch on the highlighted face.

Add a 5 mm circle at the Origin.

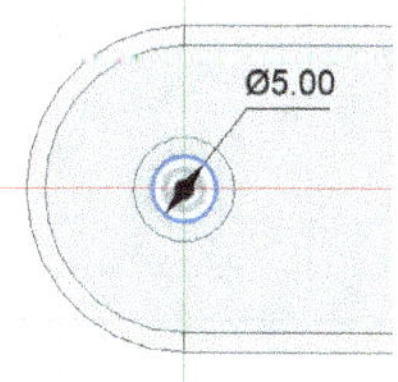

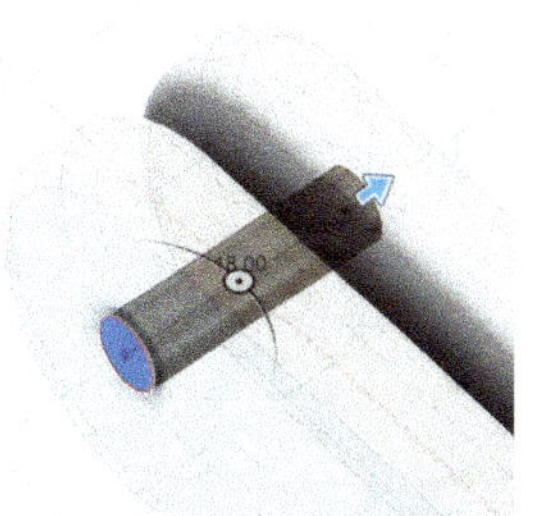

Finish the Sketch ✅ and Extrude the circle -18 mm. Add a metal appearance of your choice.

Q? Can you Extrude without entering a value?

....

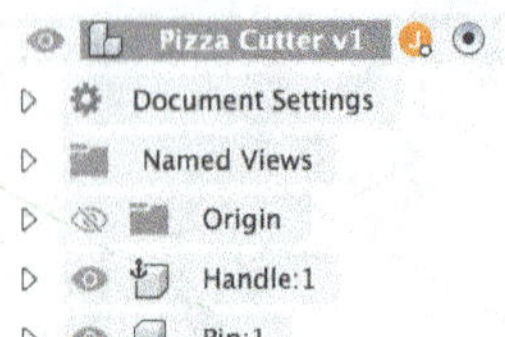

The Pin component is done! Activate the Root (top) Component in the Browser. Notice the Anchor icon next to Handle, the first component, denoting that it is Grounded or locked in place. Also notice the icons next to the components and next to the Root component.

To rigidly join the two components together, add a Rigid Joint. Because the two parts are already in the correct location, use the As-Built Joint tool found in the Assemble menu.

Verify the Joint Type is Rigid, select the Handle and the Pin, and click OK.

You can click either the Components themselves or their names in the Browser.

Q? Can you design the pin in another location and use rigid Joint?

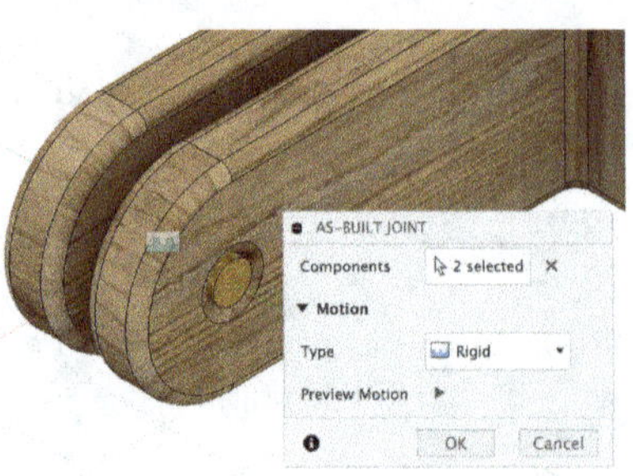

....

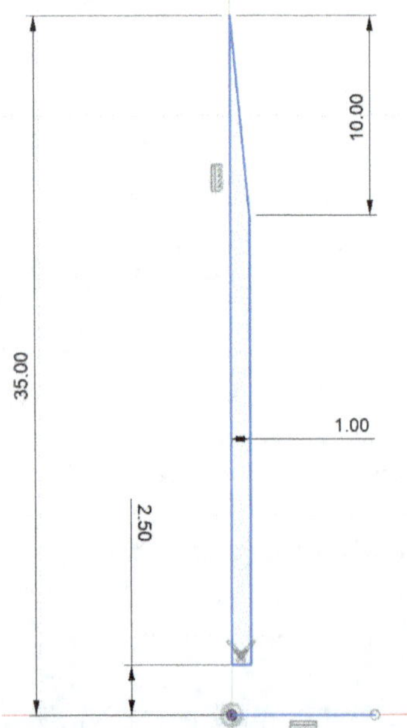

New Internal Component called Blade.

Hide the Handle and Pin Components.

New sketch, Right Plane.

Left vertical line coincident with the origin.

<< Sketch this and add the following dimensions.

Pizza Cutter 

Mirror the profile about the left vertical line and Finish the Sketch ✅.

Revolve the two profiles about the horizontal line. Add a metal of your choice and edit the settings to look better.

Q? How else could you make this blade?

....

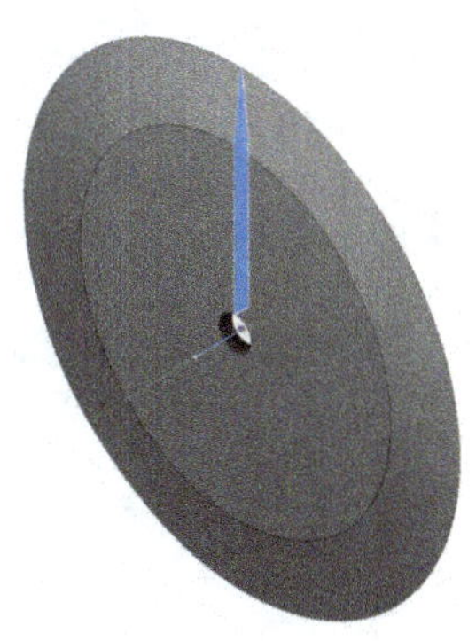

Activate the Root Component and show the other two Components.

Select the As-Built Joint tool but change the Type from Rigid to Revolute.

Select the Handle, then the Blade. The tool then asks for a Snap, or a circular edge that you want your parts to rotate about.

Click the front round edge of the Pin and the Blade will start to rotate.

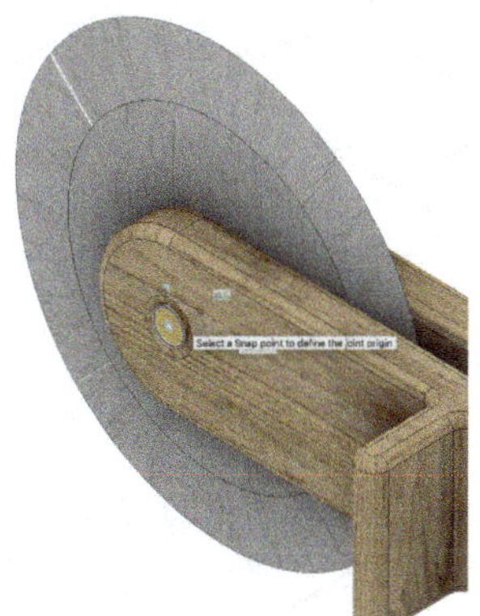

Expand Joints in the Browser, right-click Revolute 2 and select Animate Joint Relationship to animate the blade rotating.

And this project is done! 🏆

Celebrate the last project of this book with a fresh slice!

Try to design and assemble a pizza cutter starting with the pin, then the blade, then the handle. Compare and contrast the approaches - was one "better" than another?

Explore these questions and try the prompts to find out what's possible:

1. Change the type of Joint from Revolute to Cylindrical - what is the same and what is different?

2. What happens if you press the Flip button in the Edit Joint dialogue box?

3. What does holding the Command key on a Mac or Control key on a PC do when applying a Joint?

4. What does the icon for the Rigid Joint look like?

5. What is the difference between "Animate Joint" and "Animate Joint Relationship"?

6. What does the icon for the Revolute Joint look like?

7. What happens if you re-order features in the Timeline?

8. Which new terms can you fill out in the glossary in the back of the book?

Sketch a storyboard of the parts, Joints, and order of assmebly needed to recreate the movable features of a pocket knife.

Tool Review: Joints

A Joint is a relationship created between 2 Components (not Bodies) in an Assembly that defines (1) their position and (2) the permitted motion in various degrees of freedom.

The 6 DOFs (Degrees of Freedom) are **along** - translational - 3 axes (X, Y, and Z) and also **around** - rotational - each axis.

All Joints, except for Rigid, allow parts to move in a combination of these movements: rotational, linear, or both.

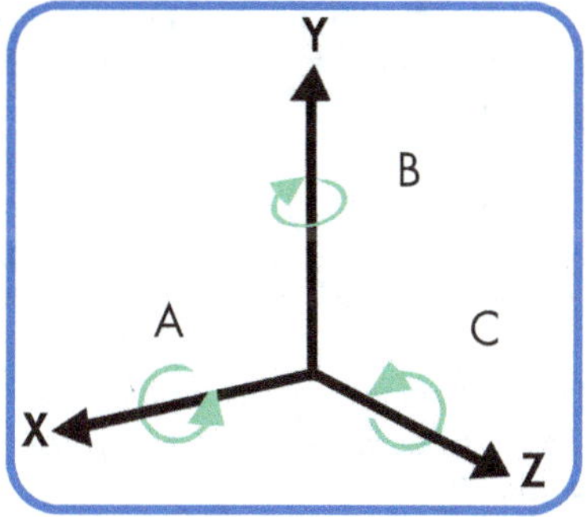

- **Rigid:** Locks 2 or more parts together. If one component is Grounded, neither will move. Example: two wooden boards glued together.
- **Revolute:** Allows a component to spin about a central Axis that can be adjusted to spin a full 360 degrees or just a part of an arc. Example: A spinning car tire on an axle.
- **Slider:** A linear movement along a single dimension. Example: a piston traveling up and down in a cylinder.
- **Cylindrical:** Allows parts to rotate and move linearly at the same time. Example: a woodworking clamp; the clamping screw mechanism requires cylindrical spinning and linear movement.
- **Pin Slot:** A component can rotate about one Axis and move linearly along a different axis. Example: A rolling pin on some pizza dough; the pin's axle is perpendicular to the direction of travel.
- **Planar:** Allows a component to rotate but is confined to only being able to move in one plane. Example: An object placed on a desk that can be moved around the desk and can rotate but can't pass through the table or be lifted upwards.
- **Ball:** A component can rotate in all 3 axes of rotation. Example: a ball Joint on top of a camera mount.

Tool Review: Assembly

An Assembly is two or more Components (not Bodies) combined into a single design. Assemblies can be created from internal components, external components, or a mix of both. 

Components can be thought of as folders that hold all the information about a part including the 3D Body, the 2D Sketches, Construction geometry to make the part, and Canvas images.

In Fusion, there are two types of components: Internal and External. Using Internal components is more common. As the name implies all the data about the component is held within the assembly file.

External components store all the parts data outside the assembly file in a folder. This frees up more computing power in the assembly file but can be tricky to work with.

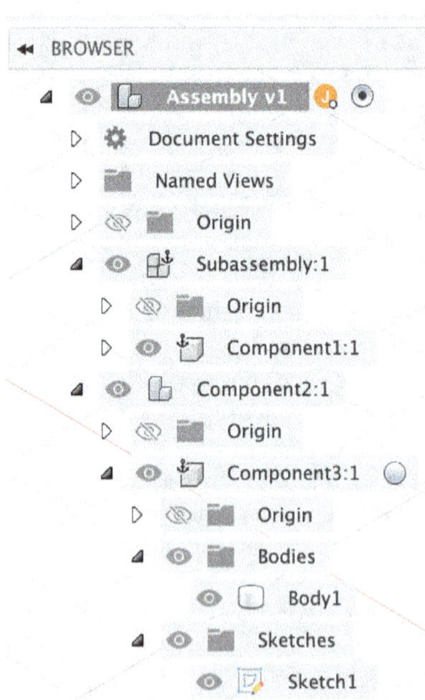

The Assembly at the top of the Browser (AKA the root component) holds all components.

You can make sub-groupings of components within the assembly called Subassemblies. Ex. If you were designing a car, you may want a subassembly for all the components in the Wheels.

Components are like folders that store information about the 3D Body, 2D sketches, and more.

You can only make Joints between Components, not Bodies, so each part of your design needs to be its own individual Component.

Before you make a new component, you must Activate the Root Component or else the previous component will become a Subassembly.

True or False?

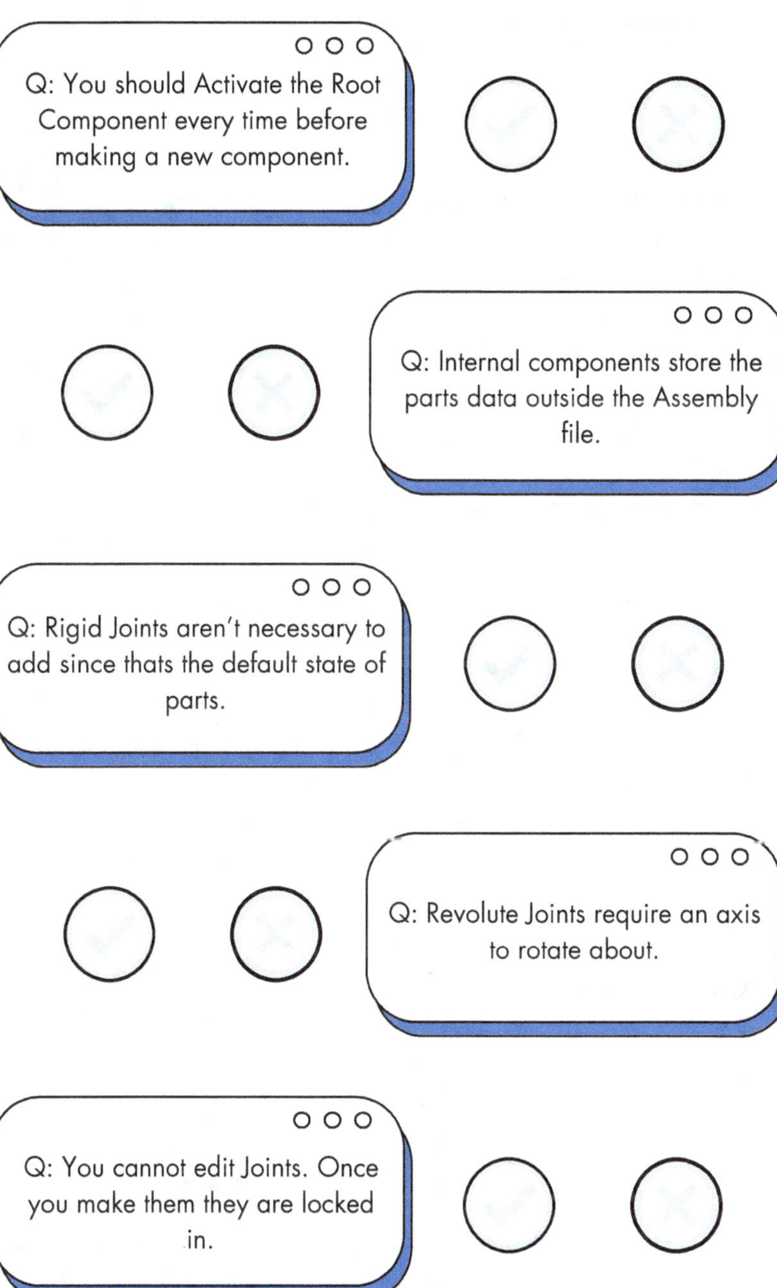

Joints Review

Match the name to the definition

Rigid

Revolute

Slider

Cylindrical

Pin Slot

Planar

Ball

- A Component can rotate in all 3 axes of rotation.
- Allows a Component to spin about a central Axis, a full 360 degrees or just a part of an arc.
- A linear movement along a single dimension. Example: a piston traveling up and down in a cylinder.
- Locks 2 or more parts together. If one Component is Grounded, neither will move.
- A Component can rotate about one Axis and move linearly along a different axis.
- Allows a Component to rotate but is confined to only being able to move in one plane.
- Allows parts to rotate and move linearly at the same time.

Challenge

Now it's time to combine your skills into a more complex and rewarding project. In this challenge, you'll design a pair of headphones from scratch. You are encouraged to use any tool that seems appropriate. (You've used Extrude, revolve, loft, and sweep.)

This is open-ended and unstructured. You are encouraged to consider how different parts can be constructed. You can make them as simple or complex as you like; the aim is to play! Let's take a look at some previous designs:

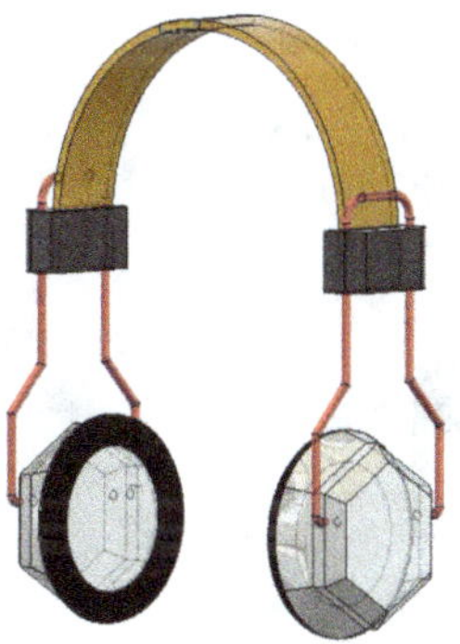

This design uses a rectangle swept along an arc to create the headband, a swept circle to create the "frame," an Extruded rectangle to create a bracket, and a hexagon lofted to a circle to make the earcups. All bodies were mirrored to make a pair of headphones.

This design uses a torus made from a revolved circle added to a cylinder made by extruding a circle. Both were mirrored. The headband is made from an Extruded sketch, with an additional spline used to make the curved feature.

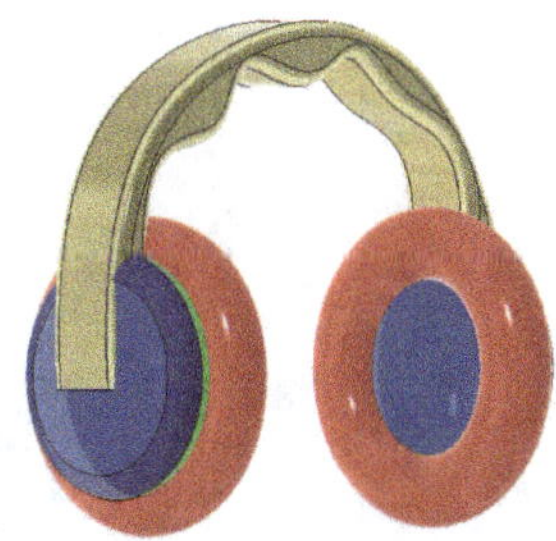

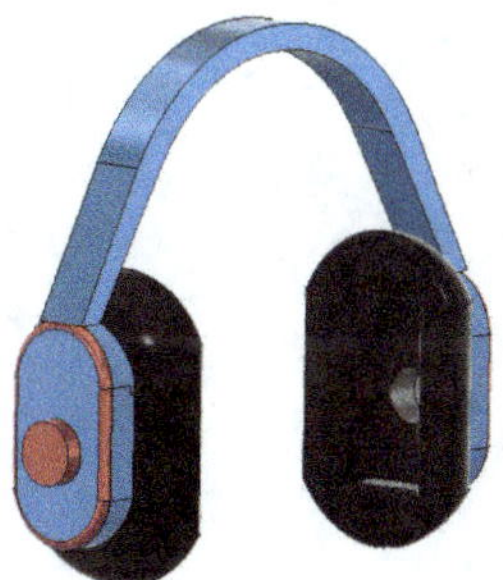

This design uses almost all Extrudes and Fillets - an arc for the headband, a cuboid for the foam, and the earcups. Again, the earcup and foam bodies were mirrored to make a pair of headphones.

Students' Headphones

Welcome to our showcase of four unique student headphone design projects!

Each of these designs reflects the creativity and skill of our students, who have taken different approaches to achieve distinct results.

From sleek minimalist concepts to bold, feature-rich designs, these headphones highlight the diverse ways students can use CAD to bring their visions to life!

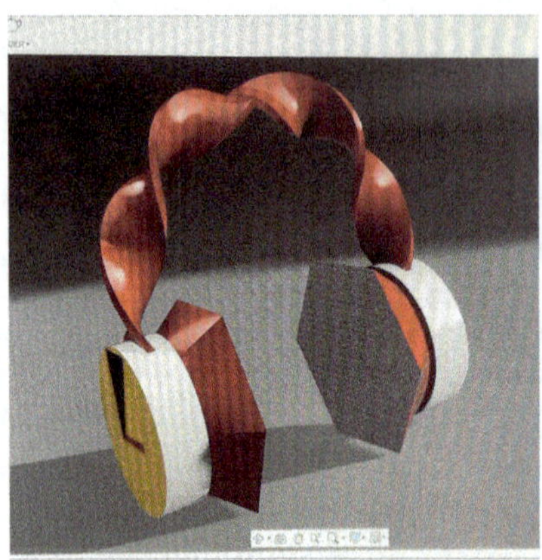

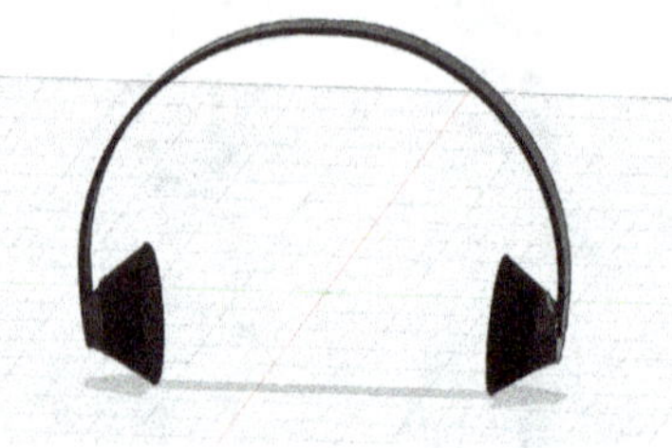

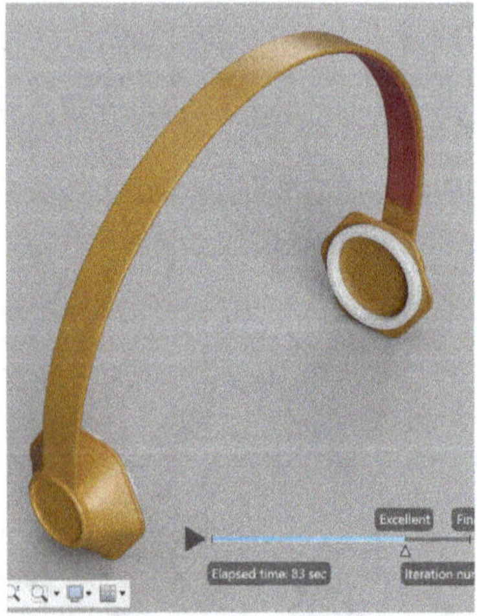

Explore Workspaces

In the following sections, you will explore other Workspaces in Fusion. Our goal is to let you know about the additional possibilities available for more advanced design work. Since this is a 12-hour starter course, step-by-step exercises are beyond the scope of this book.

If you'd like additional step-by-step practice projects, our book Mastering Autodesk Fusion has 27 amazing ones!

Visit **CADclass.org/pages/books** for a free or donation-based copy of this book and other CADclass titles.

CADclass is a platform to learn CAD, 3D printing, design, and engineering. We write books, teach online classes, and curate a worldwide community of makers. We provide free and paid resources through our social channels, website, and partner network.

Mastering Autodesk Fusion Course - Step-by-step projects in Autodesk Fusion. **CADclass.org/courses/CAD**. If you want to continue learning Fusion, this is the course for you.

Our books are available on Amazon and other platforms or for a donation/free: **CADclass.org/pages/books**

Tinkercad to Fusion

Tinkercad is another CAD software also made by Autodesk. One of the Export links in Tinkercad is called Send to Fusion, which sends your Tinkercad design straight to Fusion if you already have it installed and open.

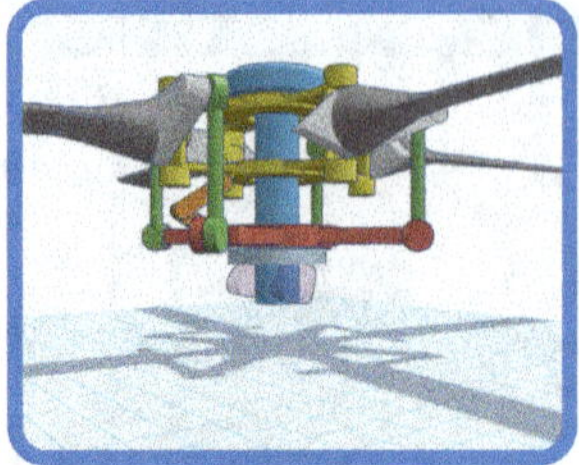
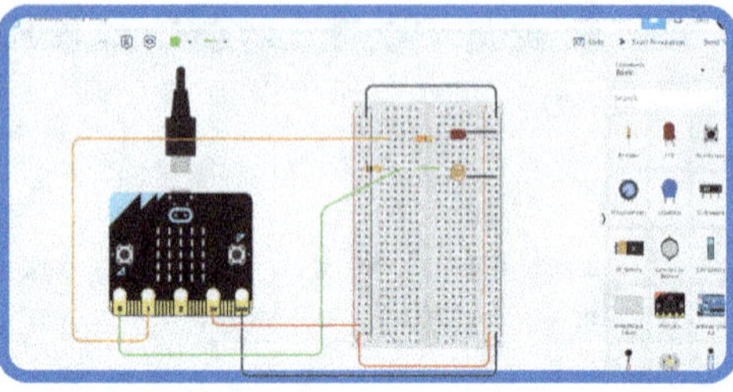

Helicopter Rotors by ZDP:
t.ly/Ek8ma

If you are interested in learning more about Tinkercad including Simlab and Tinkercad Circuits use this link to find out more:
CADclass.org

Mastering Tinkercad (Student & Instructor) - Step-by-step workbooks in Autodesk Tinkercad. If you want to start teaching or learning Tinkercad, these are the books for you.

a.co/d/fNAF2CX

Our books are available on Amazon and other platforms or for a donation/free: **CADclass.org/pages/books**

Rendering Workspace

Rendering generates a photorealistic 2D image from a 3D model. It simulates lighting, materials, and environments to create a lifelike representation of your design. This allows you to visualize how your product might look in the real world.

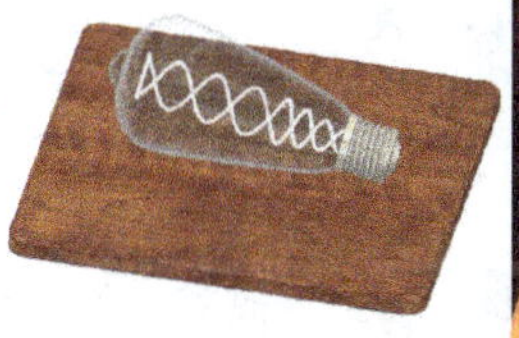
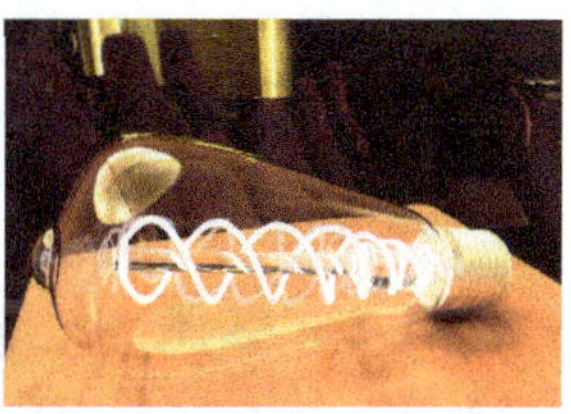

Click on the gray Design box in the top left corner and enter the Rendering Workspace to see a new Toolbar and a new rendered version of your model!

The Scene Settings tools edit the camera, the lighting, the exposure, the environment, and dozens of other settings.

The settings in this Workspace is similar to the real-life terminology with photography and videography, so if you have any experience in those fields, you will feel very comfortable here.

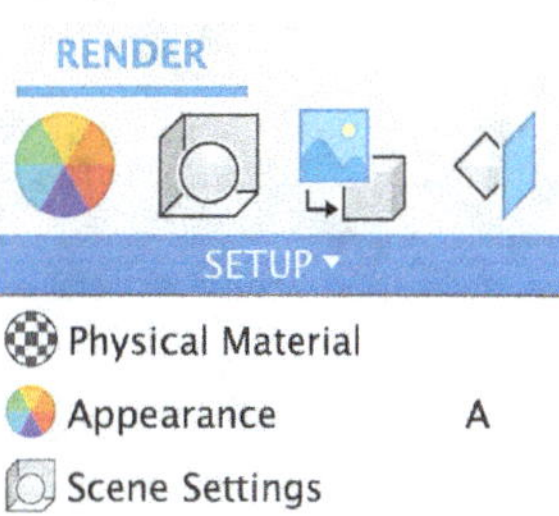

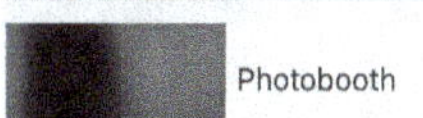

In the Rendering Workspace, you can "photograph" your project in a Studio environment or in a realistic world environment like grassy fields, sunny lake beds, Italian plazas, and dozens more.

Not only can you move your model around this world, but you can also adjust the environment to suit the mood or vibe of your project.

Rendering Workspace

Once your scene is set up to your liking, you can render the image to be photorealistic.

You have options to set the image quality size, and whether the computing happens on your computer or not.

If your machine isn't powerful enough you can, for Autodesk Cloud Credits, use their servers to process your image.

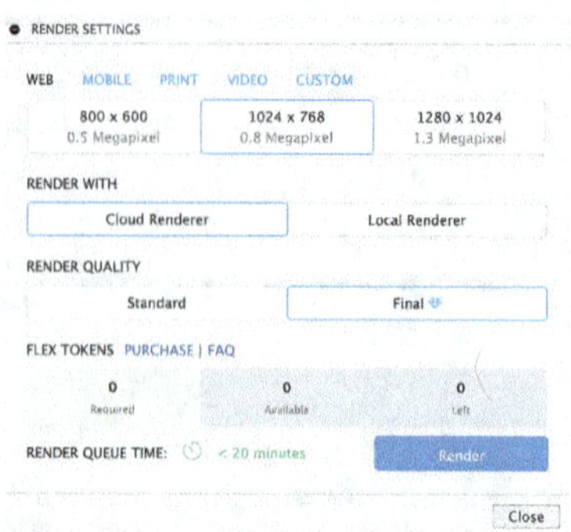

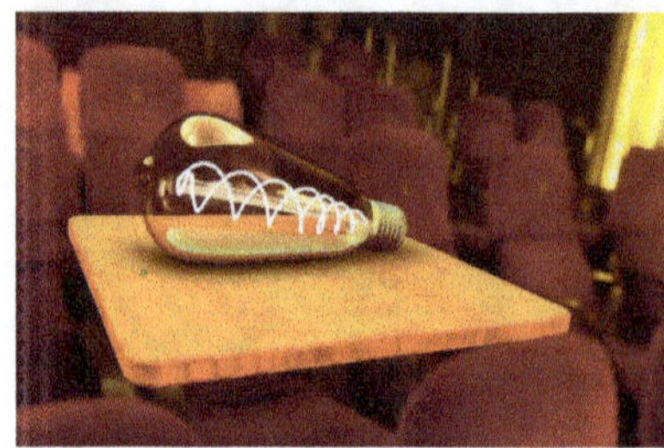

To change the background, search for a free HDRI Environment on a website like PolyHaven.com, a royalty-free page hosting hundreds of environments that you can import into your Rendering Workspace to match your project!

There are also many new AI-powered rendering tools (used to make digital designs more realistic). If you are interested, search for and try one with one of your Tinkercad creations.

These were generated in seconds in NewARC.AI

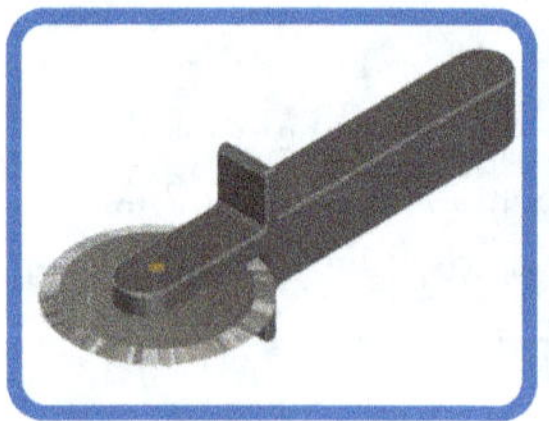

Animate Workspace

The Animation environment allows you to create dynamic visualizations of your 3D models, including motion studies, assembly/disassembly sequences, exploded views, renders, animated videos, and more.

Open the Pizza Cutter design and enter the Animation Workspace. The timeline on the bottom of the screen works similarly to a timeline in video editing software, but instead of editing clips, you edit movements of your view, zoom, linear movement and rotational movement of parts.

Move your time marker incrementally, move the camera, and move the components to show how part can be disassembled or reassembled.

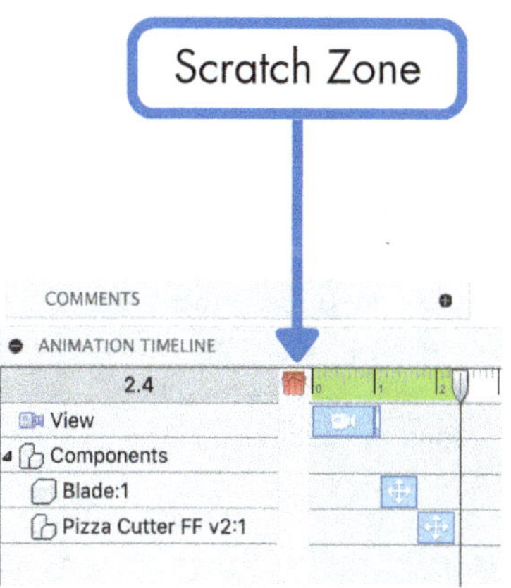

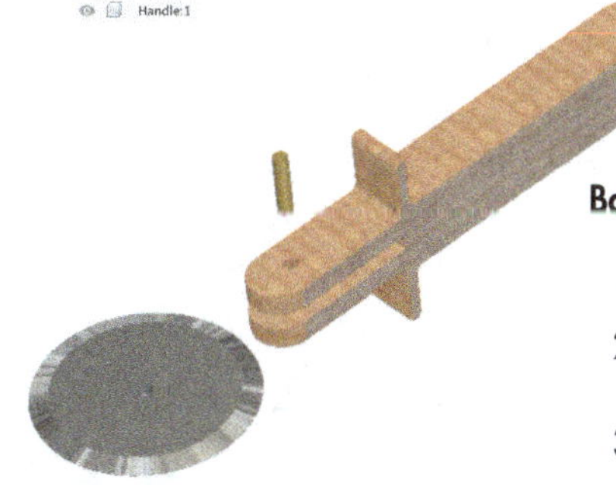

Basic Exploded Diagram:

1. Click the ViewCube faces
2. Move the playhead forward on the timeline
3. Click on the desired component and click the Transform
4. Play the animation and repeat as required

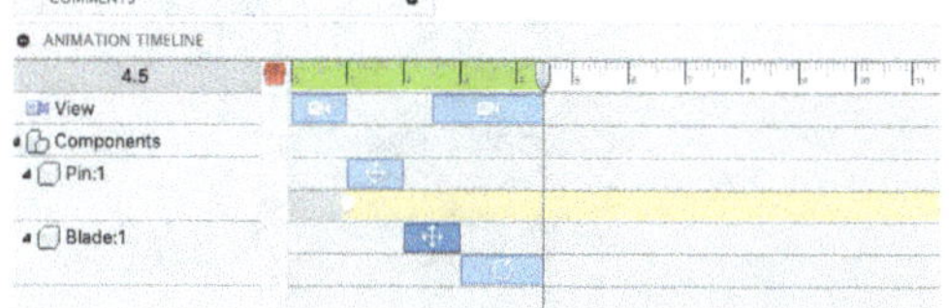

Manufacture Workspace

The Manufacturing workspace is used for CAM, including generating tool paths, simulating machining operations, creating 2D, 3D, and multi-axis milling strategies, enabling 3D printing preparation, exporting G-code, and much more.

Open the Pizza Cutter design, switch to the Manufacturing workspace, and select the Additive Tab. Next, go to the Setup menu and select New Setup.

Choose the appropriate machine for the project, then select the model you wish to work with. Once everything is set, click OK to confirm your setup.

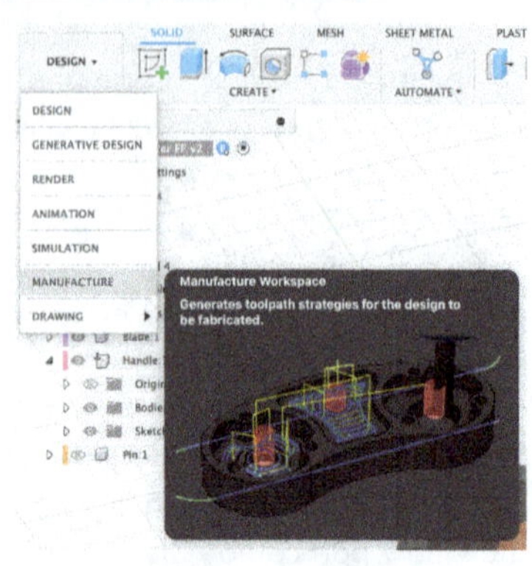

To set up your slicing parameters for 3D printing, select the layer height and the desired infill percentage.

Next, configure the support structures if needed, and decide between using brim or raft options. Once all parameters are set, generate and preview the slices to ensure everything is correct before printing. Export your g-code and print the file!

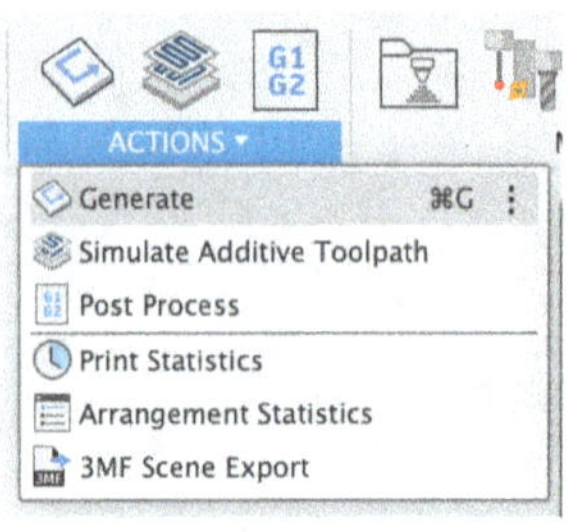

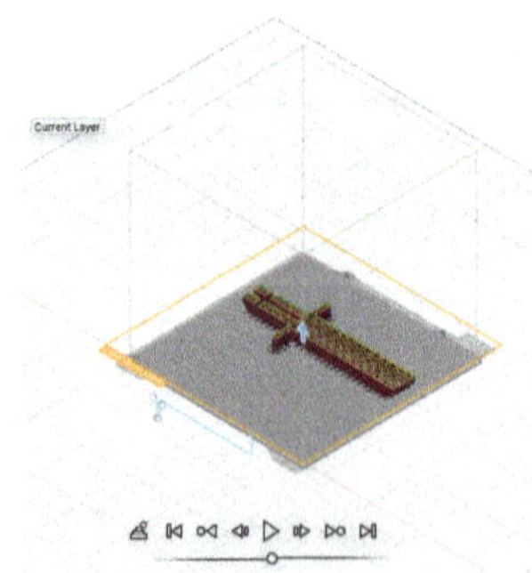

Drawing Workspace

Dimensioning a drawing is crucial for ensuring accuracy and clarity. Here are some fundamental principles to follow. There are many Dimensioning standards like ASME, Y14.5, and ISO 8015, but aim for:

1. **Clarity**: Dimensions should be easy to read and understand. Avoid crossing dimension lines.
2. **Completeness**: All dimensions should be provided to define the object completely: aim for "just enough."
3. **Consistency**: Use a consistent dimensioning style throughout the drawing, e.g. placed above and to the left.

The basic workflow is to create an engineering drawing from a 3D design:

1. Click on "Drawing" in the Workspace menu, select From Design, select sheet size, template, orientation etc.
2. Drag the part into drawing space to create the Base view, position front/main view, add additional views auto-generate from base view, arrange views with proper spacing
3. Add Dimensions/Annotations: Select Dimension tool, add critical dimensions, include any necessary notes/tolerances, add title block information, Export/Save to desired format (PDF, DWG)

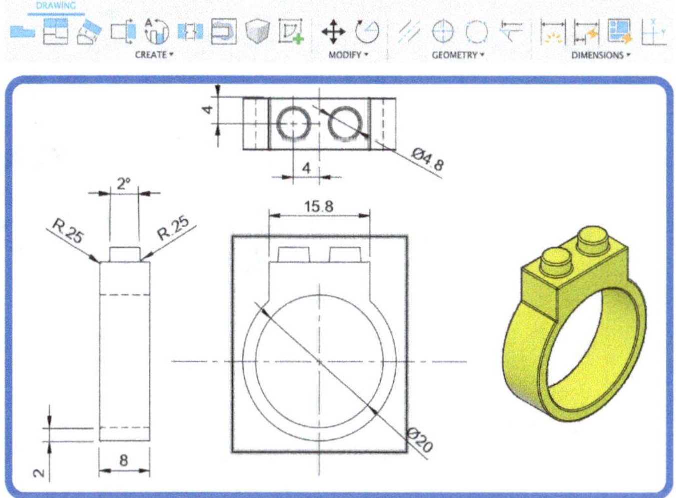

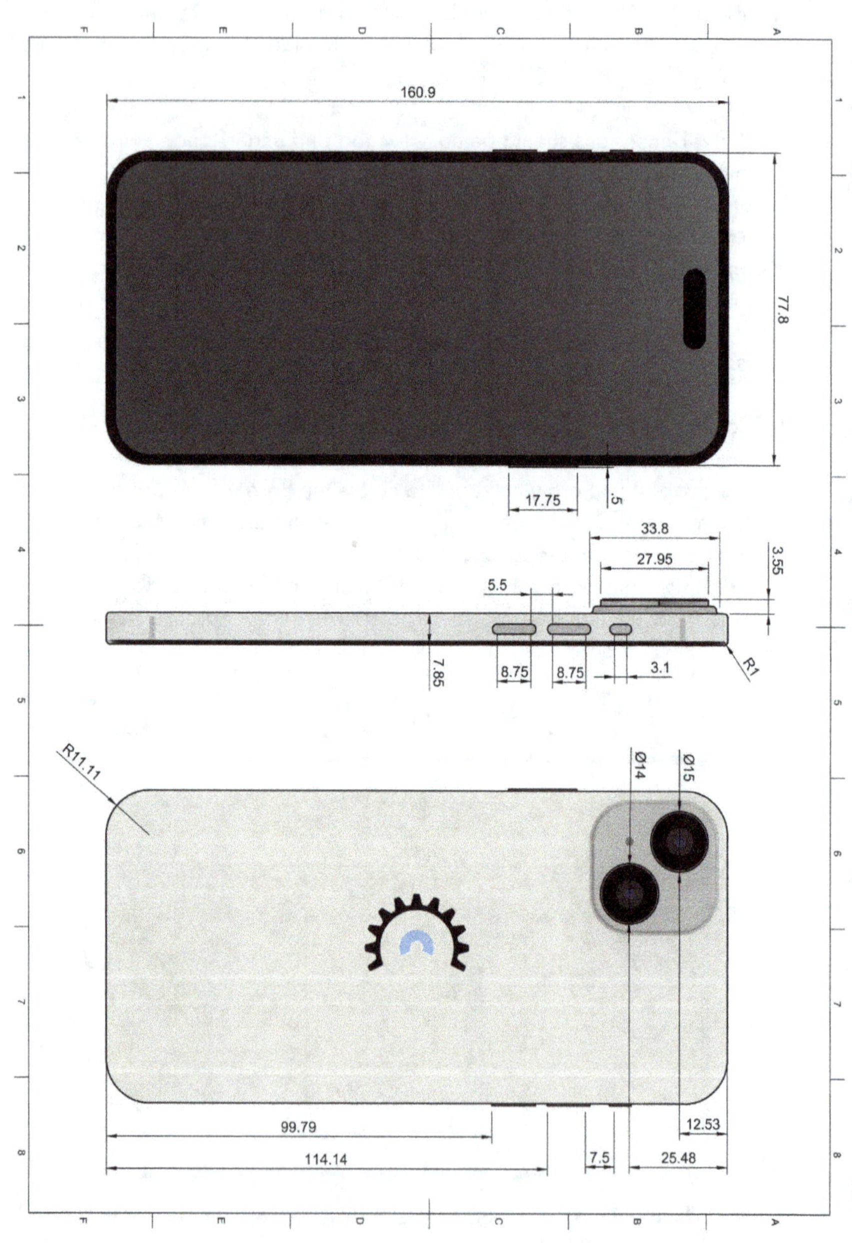
160.9
77.8
17.75
.5
33.8
27.95
3.55
5.5
7.85
8.75
8.75
3.1
R1
R11.11
Ø14
Ø15
99.79
114.14
7.5
25.48
12.53

True or False?

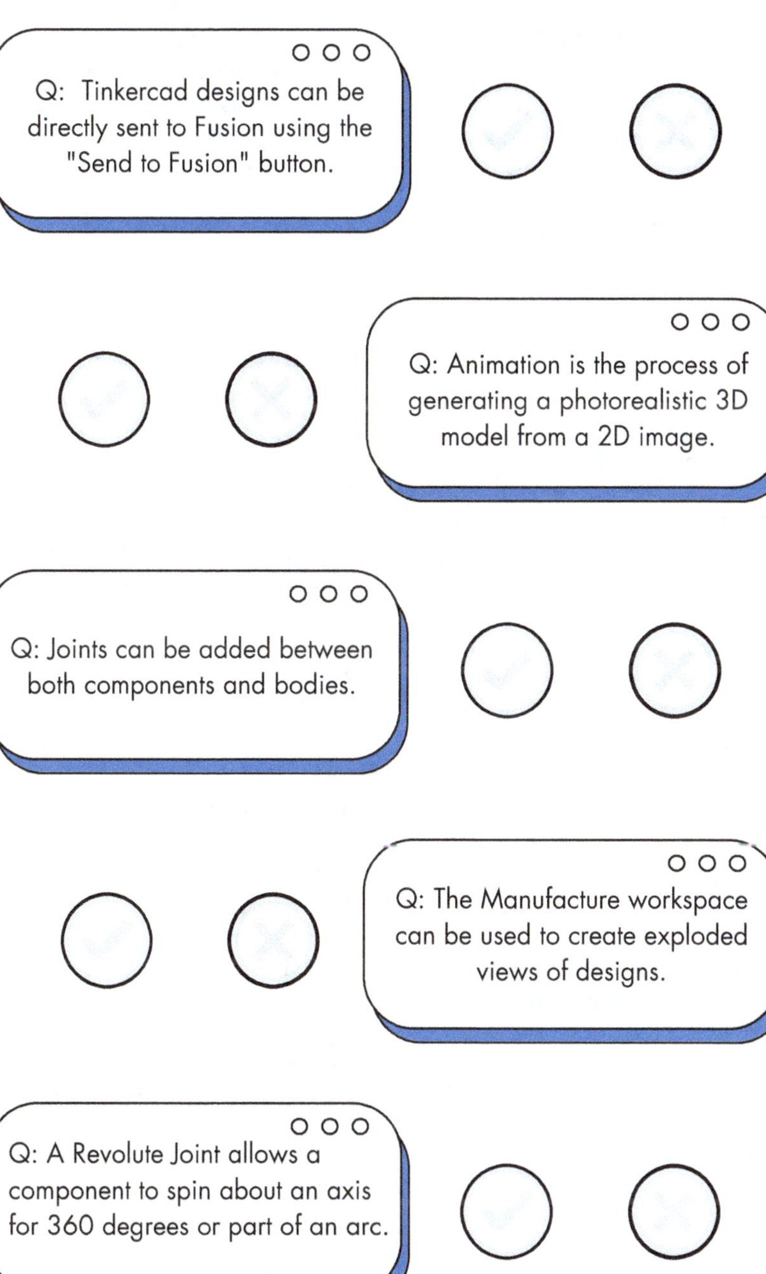

End of Book Test

1. What does CAD stand for?
- ○ Computer-Aided Drawing
- ○ Computer-Aided Design
- ○ Computer-Assisted Design
- ○ Computer-Assisted Drawing

2. Which of the following is NOT a benefit of using CAD software?
- ○ Faster design iterations
- ○ Improved design accuracy
- ○ Increased material waste
- ○ Enhanced collaboration

3. What is the name of the navigation tool located in the upper-right corner of the Fusion interface?
- ○ Timeline
- ○ Browser
- ○ ViewCube
- ○ Data Panel

4. In Fusion, what are the three primary axes representing the three dimensions?
- ○ A, B, C
- ○ L, W, H
- ○ X, Y, Z
- ○ 1, 2, 3

5. Which tool is used to create a 3D object by rotating a 2D profile around an axis?
- ○ Extrude
- ○ Sweep
- ○ Loft
- ○ Revolve

6. What is the term for a numerical value that defines the size of a design element?
- ○ Dimension
- ○ Constraint
- ○ Parameter
- ○ Variable

7. Which tool creates multiple instances of a sketch or feature in a structured arrangement?
- ○ Mirror
- ○ Offset
- ○ Pattern
- ○ Array

8. Which file format is typically used for exporting designs for laser cutting from Fusion?
- ○ .STL
- ○ .STEP
- ○ .DXF
- ○ .MP4

9. Which tool creates a 3D object by "dragging" a 2D shape along a defined path?
- ○ Extrude
- ○ Sweep
- ○ Loft
- ○ Revolve

10. Where is the hierarchical structure that organizes parts and sub-assemblies in Fusion?
- ○ Timeline
- ○ Browser
- ○ Data Panel
- ○ Feature Tree

End of Book Test

1. Name a specific piece of 'everyday' design software (not Fusion).

2. Give a unique advantage of CAD over creating designs using "traditional" hand tools like pencils and paper.

3. Explain the disadvantages of using CAD vs. designing with pencil and paper.

4. Describe 2 ways CAD could contribute to cost or time savings in design and manufacturing.

5. Explain some limitations you came up against when using Fusion.

6. How might Augmented Reality (AR) help consumers understand a product?

7. Name some benefits of designers using CAD that allow for collaboration with other designers.

8. Name the parts of a piece of clothing Fusion is well suited to design in 3D. Why is this?

9. State specific examples of types of products that Fusion is not well suited to designing in 3D. Why is this?

10. Name industries where CAD is commonly used and explain how it benefits these sectors.

11. Describe the relationship between CAD and CAM.

12. Explain the Rendering workspace as if you were talking to a 5-year-old.

13. In what way can keyboard shortcuts help a CAD designer?

14. Think up a question for your teacher/instructor:

Glossary

Sketch	....
Pan	....
Orbit	....
Extrude	....
Mirror	....
Constraint	....
Sweep	....
Loft	....
Parallel	....
Body	....
Fillet	....
Pattern	....

Glossary

Coincident ....

Shell ....

Dimension ....

Spline ....

Body ....

Revolve ....

Tangent ....

Fix ....

Workspace ....

Timeline ....

ViewCube ....

Isometric ....

Glossary

Component ....

Browser ....

Data panel ....

CAD ....

Animation ....

Render ....

2D ....

ViewCube ....

Joint ....

Version ....

3D ....

CAM ....

Shortcuts

3D Design Workspace

A: Apperance

I : Measure

S: Search Tools

H: Hole

Q: Press Pull

M: Move/Copy

E: Extrude

F: Model Fillet

V: Show/Hide

J: Joint

M: Measure

I: Window Selection

2D Sketch Workspace

R: 2-Point Rectangle

L : Line

O: Offset

D: Sketch Dimension

C: Center Diam Circle

X: Construction

P: Project

T: Trim

Resources

If you want more information on the previous Workspaces and CAD topics then consider ordering Mastering Autodesk Fusion Edt.2 available on Amazon or at **CADclass.org** for free or a donation. This much larger text includes the following:

- **Fundamentals:** Introduction of CAD modeling with Autodesk Fusion.
- **Mechanical Design:** The basics of design using manufacturing principles.
- **Parametric Design:** How to customize your designs with dimensions and parameters.
- **Assemblies:** How to build your project with multiple parts.
- **Joints:** How to join parts for realistic movement.
- **Motion Animation:** How to make your model move and come alive.
- **Appearances:** How to give your 3D models color, texture, and decals.
- **Rendering:** How to make your parts look photo-realistic.
- **Engineering Drawings:** How to make your own blueprints.
- **Exploded Diagrams:** How to explode your projects and rebuild them.
- **CAM (Computer Aided Manufacturing):** How to manufacture parts on a CNC with Computer-Aided Manufacturing.

 Be sure to check out the Make:able challenge from our good friends at PrintLab & Autodesk. 

 The **www.makeablechallenge.com** is an annual competition where students design and 3D print solutions to help people with disabilities or elderly individuals overcome everyday challenges.

Stay in touch! Email us at create@CADclass.org

Classroom Licences	Bulk Book Discounts
Curriculum Design	Bespoke Training

CERTIFICATE

Send an email to Create@CADclass.org with **"CADclass Fusion Fundamentals Certificate"** in the title to receive a digital certificate of completion!

Ed, Jake, & Josh

About CADclass

CADclass is a platform to learn CAD, 3D printing, design, and engineering. We write books, film online courses, and curate a worldwide community of makers. We provide free and paid resources through our social channels, website, and partner network.

Mastering Autodesk Fusion Course - Step-by-step projects in Autodesk Fusion. **CADclass.org/courses/CAD**. If you want to continue learning Fusion, this is the course for you.

Our books are available on Amazon and other platforms or for a donation/free: CADclass.org/pages/books

Other online courses (with free trials) are available at: **CADclass.org/pages/courses**

Socials:
Create@CADclass.org
Youtube.com/@CADclassOfficial | Tiktok.com/@cadclass
Twitter.com/cad_class | Instagram.com/cadclassofficial